caring
for the
least
of
these

caring
for the
least
of
these

SERVING CHRIST AMONG THE POOR

Edited by David Caes
Foreword by John M. Perkins

HERALD PRESS
Scottdale, Pennsylvania
Waterloo, Ontario

Library of Congress Cataloging-in-Publication Data
Caring for the least of these / edited by David Caes.
    p.   cm.
    ISBN 0-8361-3594-6 (alk. paper)
    1. Church work with the poor—United States. 2. Poor—United
States. I. Caes, David.
    BV639.P6C27 1992
    259'.08'6942—dc20   92-8755
                                                                   CIP

The paper used in this publication is recycled and meets the minimum requirements of American National Standard for Information Sciences—Permanence of Paper for Printed Library Materials, ANSI Z39.48-1984.

CARING FOR THE LEAST OF THESE
Copyright © 1992 by Christian Community Health Fellowship
    Published by Herald Press, Scottdale, Pa. 15683
    Published simultaneously in Canada by Herald Press,
    Waterloo, Ont. N2L 6H7. All rights reserved
Library of Congress Catalog Number: 92-8755
International Standard Book Number: 0-8361-3594-6
Printed in the United States of America
Design by Gwen M. Stamm

1 2 3 4 5 6 7 8 9 10 99 98 97 96 95 94 93 92

"I tell you the truth,
whatever you did
for one of the least of these . . .
you did for me."

Matthew 25:40

Contents

Foreword

OVER THIRTY MILLION Americans today do not have access to our health system. Sharing the company of South Africa as one of the world's last developed countries without national health care is an embarrassing indictment. With the ground swell of discontent over rising health care costs, and politicians tripping over one another with blueprints for solving the anger, finally the crisis is receiving its due attention.

Caring for the Least of These rises above the fray of "quick-fix" proposals for our health care and social welfare crises. As their graphic stories from the front lines of our ghettos and barrios show, the authors have long been too familiar with the disgraceful failures of our health care institutions, other social systems, even our churches.

This book's cries from overlooked places of need show dramatically the inefficiency of our present social service delivery system. We hear in this book the agony of the least of these who have been long ignored.

But theirs is more than a cry of concern—it is a cry of hope. For these stories show us the courage and compassion of Christians—poor people, social workers, doctors, nurses, and administrators—living and working in desperate places to gain or provide quality, affordable services.

Because they are close to the problems, the authors show us that the issue is not just providing care. It is providing hope. It is wishing and working to see the least of these experience the same wholeness we wish for ourselves and our families.

Their call is more than just skin-deep. It goes beyond more beds or doctors or money to ask how social needs can become territory introducing the poor to the Great Physician who enables us to "take up your mat and walk." *Caring for the Least of These* shows that there is a need for social organizations which affirm the dignity of our people and create the incentives and motivation that lead to long-term development.

The time is right for committed Christians to say "Yes!" to social justice for all. It is time for Christians, through their concern for the deepest wholeness in life, to show our nation a way out of our present distress.

My prayer is that you who read this book will be inspired and challenged to roll up your sleeves and obey the command of Jesus: "For as much as you have done it to the least of these, my disciples, you have done it unto me."

—*John Perkins*
Pasadena, California

Editor's Preface

IMAGINE YOU were planning to go to Italy as a missionary. Before you left, you might visit your local library to borrow every book available on Italy. You would probably call the tourism bureau to ask for material on traveling in Italy. You would ask friends or relatives who had been in Italy what you should expect. When you arrived in Italy, you would expect to spend at least a year learning Italian. After all, how could you communicate effectively with Italians if you didn't even know their language?

I grew up in Italy, where my parents are missionaries. I have met many missionaries and am impressed by the preparations many of them make for their work. Sending a missionary overseas requires a lot of money, so you want to make sure the investment is a wise one. Time spent reading about the country and its culture is well spent. Italian social customs are different from United States practices, and learning about the differences could spare you embarrassing moments.

Although I grew up in Italy, I came back to the United States to go to college. Since graduating some fifteen years ago, I have lived and worked in inner-city communities in the United States. While there are tremendous needs overseas, I decided I could not in good conscience turn my back on the incredible needs that exist in my own country.

In the last fifteen years, I have seen many people come and go. They see the needs that exist in our poor inner-city and rural communities and decide they will do things *for* people who live there. Typically, these are well-intentioned white Christians who decide to work in African-American, Hispanic, Native American, Asian, or Appalachian communities. They may be in their native country, but they are working in a culture that is not their own.

They survive for a year or two, then burn out and return to the more affluent communities from which they came. They seem genuinely perplexed by the people they wanted to work with. They make friends with a lot of children—but don't develop meaningful friendships with adults. They leave feeling they had a lot to offer the poor—but are now overwhelmed and rejected.

As I run across these people, I am struck by how well-intentioned yet ignorant and uninformed they are. They have not read about the culture of the people with whom they seek to work. They do not understand the customs. They have not sought out those who are living and working among the poor. They have not listened to the people they claimed to serve. They did not do their homework.

But not everyone burns out and leaves. Some remain, struggle, listen, struggle some more. They find ways to live out God's calling in their lives. In these pages, you will find their stories. All of this book's contributors are members of the Christian Community Health Fellowship—a national network of Christian health professionals and others who are concerned about the health care needs of the poor in the United States. They speak from experience, both in ministering as well as receiving ministry.

Special mention should be made here of Kathleen Hayes. As associate editor of this book, she ensured that each contributor's material flowed smoothly and contributed to the book's continuity. Eddy Hall deserves equal recognition for careful copy editing.

The purpose of this book is to give those of you interested in working among the poor some basic tools for living out your calling. Although the book does not give information about working with particular cultural groups, it highlights issues involved in working among poor people in any setting.

Do not expect this book to romanticize or glorify working among poor people. Expect it instead to help you face more realistically the unique challenges of serving the poor. Expect it to make you uncomfortable. Expect it to bring you to greater understanding and faithfulness to God. Above all, expect to learn valuable lessons from those who are poor as well as from middle-class Christians who have heeded God's call to "care for the least of these."

—David Caes, Executive Director
Christian Community Health Fellowship
P.O. Box 12548
Philadelphia, PA 19151-0548

Part I

The Experiences of Being Poor

AS CHRISTIANS, many of us have a desire to serve poor people. We have probably all had conversations about the needs of the poor. Maybe we even talk a lot about the poor and how to help them. It may be easy for us to conclude that the poor in our inner cities need better access to a health care system or better schools.

Yes, we talk *about* the poor. But how often do we talk *with* them and listen to their stories? What do the people whom we call "the poor" feel *they* need the most? Are we willing to listen to those we are seeking to serve? Are we willing to learn what it means to walk in their shoes?

It is easy to condemn the poor for the choices they have made—much easier than to listen, to understand, then to help. In responding to the gospel's challenge to care for "the least of these," it is crucial to listen.

So we begin by giving you the opportunity to listen to people from impoverished communities talk about their own experiences of poverty and well-intentioned benevolence. You will also hear about one middle-class family's frustrating experience with trying to meet a human need. Please listen. It is the first and vital step toward helping the poor.

1. Sick of Being Poor

by Teresa Maldonado

I WOKE UP early one morning with strong pains in my stomach. As I lay in bed, the pain would come and go. When it came, I doubled over and broke out in a sweat. My husband was out of town, and I was at home with my five children. After about an hour, I realized I had to do something.

I thought about what I could do. I thought of walking to one of the medical clinics just around the corner from my house, but we were broke. I thought of going to a hospital emergency room, but we didn't have health insurance. If I couldn't pay a doctor, I certainly couldn't pay a hospital emergency room bill either. My only remaining choice was to go to the Board of Health Clinic.

I panicked. Although I was a registered patient there and had taken my children there many times, I had gone there only once or twice for myself. I was afraid because I knew I needed help, yet I knew that getting into the clinic might not be easy.

If I called and made my condition sound too serious,

they would say, "Honey, don't come in. You're too sick. Go straight to the hospital." If I didn't communicate how sick I was, they would say, "Sure you can come in. How about a week from Friday?"

The pain was too intense to ignore, so I took a deep gulp and called. A gentleman in the Adult Medicine department answered. I explained my situation and asked for permission to come in. His response was, "You've called the wrong place. You belong in Family Planning."

Family Planning! The effort I was making to hide my pain kept me from blowing up. "I know the difference between my stomach and my uterus," I said. He got flustered and put me on hold.

Within a few minutes a nurse was on the line. I had to start all over. When I was through, she said the same thing: "You belong in Family Planning."

"I am a registered patient with Adult Medicine. I do not belong in Family Planning," I repeated. "I'm not going to have any more babies. Please let me come in."

The nurse put me on hold again. When she came back, she was clearly annoyed with me. I could not come in until 1:00 p.m., she said. And if I did come in, she wouldn't guarantee I would see the doctor, even if I waited until closing time that evening.

After hanging up, I decided my pain wasn't bad enough to be worth enduring such treatment all day. I was powerless. I never did go in. The pain eventually subsided.

To be poor is to be powerless, to be boxed in, to have no choices. The professionals who live and work in my community are there by choice. They have the option of walking away into the regular job market and earning more somewhere else. The very fact that professionals are providing services implies a position of power. Such people are not poor, no matter how frugally they may choose to live.

Those of us who receive those services are powerless, perhaps because we lack education, good communication skills, or marketable job skills. We cannot walk away from our neighborhood into the land of success and prosperity.

The health care system illustrates the lack of options for the poor. I am forced to seek health care for myself and my children in a system that is dehumanizing, impersonal, belittling, and blaming.

Health Care Which Dehumanizes

A typical visit to the Board of Health Clinic includes at least six, and sometimes as many as ten, lines to wait in. When one of my children gets sick and I call to ask permission to bring my child in, I brace myself for a three- to five-hour ordeal.

When I arrive, I go to the nurse's desk and wait my turn. When I see the nurse, I assure her that I called and let her know that I have arrived. She puts a check next to my name and sends me to the records counter.

I then wait my turn to get my records. When I receive my child's medical records, I shuffle back to the nurse's station and wait my turn again. She pulls out a computer sheet that will be filled out by every person who sees my child and attaches it to the records.

I go back to the first desk to see the person who will prepare my bill. I go to the other side of the clinic and wait my turn to pay the fee. Next I go to a waiting room to get my child's weight and temperature checked.

After that I gather everything together and wait in the waiting room for the doctor. If the doctor feels a lab test is necessary, I go to the lab. I have to wait longer there than in all the other lines combined. When I am through at the lab, I go back to the doctor and wait for her to see me again.

If the doctor feels a prescription and follow-up visit are needed, I must go to the other side of the center to wait for my prescription, then back to the records counter for the clerk to give me another appointment.

Through all this I am juggling my infant and two toddlers as I shuffle from line to line. If it is winter, I'm also toting four sets of hats, coats, scarves, and gloves. As if there weren't enough waiting in line already, during my first visits I got in wrong lines several times.

By the time I leave the clinic, I feel exhausted, disgusted, and worthless. At every station I have had to endure intolerance, indifference, and impatience from those "helping" me. Through body language, tone of voice, or lack of eye contact, I get the message loud and clear that I am a nobody. It seems every time I go in at least one person is angry with me for daring to ask for service. When a child is sick, my only choices are to endure this treatment or decide that I can't handle it that day and stay home with my sick child.

When you have to go through this dehumanizing process time after time, it eventually becomes a part of you. You begin to believe you really *are* nobody.

When I shared my experiences with a friend, she pointed out that Dr. Martin Luther King, Jr., had said, "They no longer have to tell us to go to the rear of the bus; we will fight to get there." In other words, when you are treated like that again and again, it becomes a part of your being, and you begin to do only what is expected of you.

Health Care Which Is Impersonal

When I go to the corner store, the grocer knows me, my children, and my husband. She knows my neighbors and their families. If I haven't been to each of the businesses in our neighborhood at least a dozen times, I have passed them on my way to the others. If I don't know the owners by name, I at least know them by sight. I know them and they know me.

During the warm weather we live outside our houses as much as we do inside. I have a neighbor who always sits outside his house. He is our neighborhood patriarch—a solid, consistent fixture. I see him whenever I get my mail. I see him when I go outside to call my children. I see him when I open my door to see what the weather is like. He knows everybody—who they are, where they live, who lives with them, and what is going on in their lives.

Impersonal service is foreign to my community, where I know I belong. But this security withers when I have to go to the Women, Infants, and Children program (WIC), the Public Aid office, or the Board of Health Clinic. Once inside these offices, I am anonymous. I become a number, and that anonymity hurts.

When I am in touch with that pain, all I want to do is run out and go home. Whatever I am there to get doesn't seem worth it. I avoid those places if at all possible. After two years on WIC, I got to the point where I couldn't stand the dehumanizing treatment any more; I gave up my benefits.

Health Care Which Belittles

When I go to the clinic, any of ten doctors could be on duty. The doctor doesn't know me and may not see me again for a year. To the doctor, I am just another face.

Because I don't have money, I am treated as though I cannot think for myself or make appropriate choices for my family. It would seem that relating to a child's mother would be a key part of diagnosing the child's illness. After all, I know my child better than she does. But when I say, "I think my child has this," the doctor doesn't listen and treats me as if I don't count.

I don't go to the clinic unless my child is very sick, so that at least they will believe me when I say my child is ill. I have a daughter who just turned five years old. Before her third birthday, she had pneumonia twelve times. She never had a cold or flu; whenever she got sick she got pneumonia, and that would eventually be verified at the clinic.

After her second or third bout with pneumonia, I began to recognize the symptoms. I would call for permission to go into the clinic and plan on being there for three to five hours. I thought going in before the pneumonia got bad was the responsible thing to do.

Each time all I would hear was, "Yes, your daughter has a fever. Yes, she is coughing. But no, she does not have pneumonia."

In my mind I'd say, *Yes, but give her a day or two.* I'd get Sudafed and Tylenol and be sent home. Two days later, my daughter would be sicker. I would have to hold my limp, little girl in my arms while I tried to work the system. That is powerlessness.

One year we actually had health insurance. When our daughter started to have trouble breathing one evening, my husband and I were pleased to realize we didn't have to wait until the next day to go to the clinic —we could take her to the hospital emergency room for a shot of adrenaline. After the doctor finally examined her two hours later, he said she had asthma and gave her a shot. He also said she had a touch of pneumonia; he wanted to hospitalize her.

That confused me. Hospitalize her for a touch of pneumonia? I said that I knew how to take care of her at home. My husband said there was no way we would leave her in the hospital because all they would do was give her an antibiotic and some Tylenol. We said no.

The doctor left. When he came back five minutes later, he dropped a bomb. "We think your daughter has cystic fibrosis." What could we do? We gave in and let them hospitalize her.

My husband and I took turns staying with her days and evenings. By the fifth day, we still had not seen the doctor. He somehow managed to examine my daughter in the ten minutes it took one of us to get a sandwich. She was never tested for cystic fibrosis.

When we called the doctor, he said, "I don't have confidence in this hospital's ability to test for cystic fibrosis. When I release her, I'll give you an order, and you can take her to Children's Memorial Hospital."

My daughter was in the hospital for ten days. During that time she got Tylenol regularly and an antibiotic every eight hours. A respiratory therapist came and pounded on her back once a day. I could have done that! When we got the bill, the insurance company refused to pay $3,000 because it was a preexisting condition. This kind of experience is belittling.

Health Care Which Blames the Victim

When our children get sick, we parents naturally feel responsible. But when we take our children in for care, it is devastating to be told it is all our fault.

When my son was six months old, he got a high fever. When I took him in, I found out he had an ear and throat infection. That infection and fever seemed to last until after his first birthday. As I think back on that time, my only memories are of being in the bathroom with my son in the tub (trying to bring his fever down), or at the doctor's office getting him a prescription for an antibiotic. Toward the end of those six months, the doctor looked me squarely in the face. He said if I could not get my child well and keep him well, he was going to have my son taken away from me.

Now I know children get sick in the suburbs. Why else would there be so many pediatricians and hospitals out there? Do the pediatricians in the suburbs blame the child's mother every time a child is sick? Do pediatricians in the suburbs threaten to take a child away from its mother because the child is sick? Why am I always to blame when my child is sick? I am told that the decisions I make, the food I prepare, the way I dress my children, and where we live is all my fault. That is why my child is sick.

When I was asked to share my experiences, I was afraid. What if people agreed with the doctor at the clinic? But as I was working on this, I showed it to some of my neighbors and relatives. As they read about my experiences, their mouths fell open. They were amazed that I had been able to name something deep inside of them—something that was tearing them up. "That's me," they said. "Go ahead and say it."

So I decided to risk it. And what I have to say is that most of the time the health care system's treatment of the poor in this country is dehumanizing, impersonal, belittling, and blaming. But it doesn't have to be. Empowered by God's Spirit, people can learn to serve the poor with compassion and without paternalism.

Teresa Maldonado lives with her family in Chicago, Illinois.

2. Farewell to Welfare

by Cheryl Hodges

I HAVE NEVER MET a happy welfare recipient. Some people assume that welfare recipients enjoy receiving $200 checks each month. For me, being on welfare was devastating. You couldn't pay me enough to get me to go back on it.

Just filling out welfare applications was humiliating. The questions I had to answer were unbelievable. I am not from a poor community. My dad was a hard-working man who owned a dry cleaners. We were never rich, but he adequately provided for our family. I grew up working in that cleaners and knew what hard work was about.

Many people asked me why I didn't take any job I could get, even if it paid only minimum wage. Of course, I would have preferred to be working. But with two children, I couldn't take just any job. I had to earn enough to pay for day care. Also, many jobs don't offer medical benefits, while welfare offers at least some coverage through Medicaid. Compared to a minimum-wage job, my family was better off financially on welfare. So, much as I hated it, for my family's sake I applied for welfare.

I learned quickly that there are unspoken rules about how a poor person should act. When you go to the welfare office, if you use words longer than one syllable, someone will comment, "You seem to be an intelligent person. Why aren't you working?" I was asked that question countless times. I also learned never to smile or move too quickly in a food stamp line. Otherwise people would think I was up to no good and intended to sell my food stamps.

While I was on welfare, I was outside the mainstream of society. Society passed me by. I did not exist as an individual, only as a statistic. I became dependent on a society that did not know me—and did not want to know me.

Welfare perpetuates feelings of poverty and hopelessness. After one year on welfare—the first of five—I realized I did not have the means to get off welfare. The welfare system is so overpowering that you almost need supernatural means to escape it.

Welfare and lines go hand-in-hand. Every time I visited the welfare or employment offices, I stood in line, sometimes for hours. Lines never move quickly. Nothing is more humiliating than being poor and feeling indebted to the government, but if I was going to support my family, that was what I had to do.

Every few weeks I had to visit the office of the Work Incentive Program (WIN) and look through a listing of jobs that no one I ever saw there was qualified for. I was trained as a paralegal, but I never saw a paralegal position listed. Once I saw a position as a sandwich maker. I thought surely I was qualified to make sandwiches, but they wanted someone with three years experience!

One of the hardest things I did was grocery shopping. Every time I got in line in the grocery store, I would have to pull out my food stamps and tear them out of the booklet. Other people in line would look in my grocery basket to see what I was buying. I could hear people say, "No wonder the system is going down the tubes—she's drinking her money in Pepsi." Or they would make derogatory remarks about my buying lean beef instead of regular ground beef. To minimize embarrassment, I learned to shop at 7:00 a.m.

Welfare recipients are constantly accused of being dishonest, even though it doesn't pay to be honest. Each month I had to file a monthly status report of any income or cash gifts I received. If someone gave me five dollars, I had to report it. If a client owned a car, the technician would interrogate the client to find out where it came from. Some good friends of mine gave me a car. I knew that if I told my technician how I got it, he would never believe me.

My father is a disabled veteran. Through him I was able to receive veteran's benefits for schooling. The social service system went out of its way to make it difficult for me to reach my goal of finishing school. My technician assumed that since I was getting an education, I was up to no good.

The welfare system cannot tolerate people who have goals. While I was in school, I got threatening letters from social services, accusing me of pilfering their funds. School was stressful enough, but this added harassment made me want to drop out. I did finish, but in the interim, social services said that I owed them $1,000—a number they pulled out of the air. I had to go for a hearing, but since they had no proof I owed them any money, charges were dropped. The one way

I was able to stand up to the system while I was on welfare was at that hearing.

While I was on welfare, nothing really happened in my life. I am a creative person, but while I was in the welfare system, I could not be creative. Nothing stimulated me to dream. Nothing moved me to explore. My mind rotted from lack of stimulation. I became a nonperson.

When I started working part-time for the Inner City Health Center, I stayed on welfare. That, I discovered, is taboo. But I still needed the welfare benefits; without them I would have been worse off than if I hadn't been working at all. During that time my income was constantly monitored, and my case worker made me feel guilty for taking the welfare money.

I never could have gotten off welfare on my own. But my church subsidized my salary for six months, and Inner City Health Center offered me a job. I am now the office manager.

Even though jobs and money do not provide meaning in life, they did free me from bondage. I no longer have to report to welfare workers who assume I'm dishonest because I'm poor. I no longer have to go through the motions of looking for work through an "employment" office that offers only dead-end leads. I no longer have to cringe when I pay for my groceries. I am no longer just a number. I am a person again.

Every day I see women in the same situation I was in. Sometimes it's hard for me to look at them because I know what they're going through. Even though it brings up painful memories I'd rather forget, I often tell these women I was on welfare. The Lord uses my experience to open doors. They know I understand what they're going through, and many times they listen.

Even though I know how hard it is to escape the system, I still find it easy to be cold and calloused toward women on welfare. Sometimes I get angry with them when what they really need is encouragement. They need people to understand how devastating being on welfare can be. They need people to understand that they are victims of a system that often penalizes them for working. They need people to be patient with them as they try to make their way out of the welfare system. They need choices. They need options that come only when they get viable jobs.

By myself, I never would have made it. But with God's help and the help of God's people, I did. I am grateful to the Lord for enabling me to say farewell to welfare.

Cheryl Hodges lives in Denver, Colorado, with her two daughters.

3. Victimized by Benevolence

by Teresa Maldonado

AS A CHILD, I never went to bed hungry. I was never homeless. But I knew I was poor. Nothing on television ever matched what I knew as life, but I didn't need TV to know I was poor. I knew people who were worse off than I was, but most (even my own relatives) were better of.

My parents were born in Puerto Rico and migrated as adults to Chicago, where they met and married. My father completed the sixth grade and my mother the ninth. They were both unskilled factory laborers, and many times only one was employed.

Because of my ethnic background and because we were poor, my mother did the doctoring in our home. I'm not talking about herb teas or poultices or home remedies. No, my mother was the doctor.

My community was of mixed ethnicity, and almost all were the first generation to live in the United States. What my mother did must have been common because it was easy for her to go to the pharmacy and buy prescription drugs without a prescription. She would buy penicillin, syringes, and needles. Whenever one of us seven children had a fever and failed to hide it from her, her solution was an enema. That was the cure-all. When the enema didn't work, we got a shot.

When I was fourteen years old, I had a high fever. My mother gave me a shot, but I got worse. My temperature went from 102 to 104 degrees. I remember being delirious. I remember how nervous she got, and I remember other people being in our home, though I don't know why they were there.

As I lay on the couch, completely wrapped up in blankets like a papoose, I heard the adults whispering. "My God," one of them said, "she's got to be taken to the hospital." Then someone else said, "Yeah, but if you do, you'll be put in jail for giving her a shot."

I remember being very afraid—afraid for myself and afraid for my mother. Thankfully, my fever broke and I didn't have to go to the doctor or the hospital.

There *were* doctors in our community. In fact, within two blocks, there were about six storefront clinics. The doctors were all Hispanics from different Latin American countries. Their fees, though, were outrageous. Twenty, twenty-five years ago my mother was paying $20 to $25 just for an office visit. Then the doctor would always order X-rays, shots, and prescriptions— to be done in his office or filled by his own pharmacy. It wasn't uncommon for my mother to pay $100 for just one office visit. Because she had a chronic medical condition, she was forced to go to the doctor herself, but she couldn't afford it for all of us.

Later I learned that much of the physician's income came from public aid. It seems that the government permitted him to charge an inordinate rate, as long as it was applied across the board. The private patients were overcharged to protect government reimbursements. I found out that the fees he charged were the same he charged public aid patients. He couldn't get away with charging two different fees, so everyone had to pay what he was charging the government.

I married young. I was seventeen. It was the thing to do back then. I had already graduated from high school and had even attended college for one year. I was nineteen when I had my first child. When I was twenty-one, I became a Christian. God was gracious and saved Ray, my husband, the same year. We were both ignorant about the Christian way of life. We knew nothing. We had no idea who David or Daniel were. I can't tell you how surprised I was when I found out that Samson was in the Bible.

When Ray was called into the ministry, he enrolled in Bible college to make up for that void in our lives. We then took a leap of faith: he quit his job. We went from two incomes, which allowed us to live comfortably, to my one.

At age twenty-five, poverty once again became a way of life for me. The cost of child care and the other expenses of my working reduced my salary to a net of about a dollar an hour. My job required me to be out of the home about fifty hours a week. We were all miserable. We just couldn't manage it. So I quit my job to care for the children. Since Ray was still a full-time student, his part-time job provided our only income.

When somebody told us we would probably qualify for food stamps, we decided to apply. The caseworker said we qualified for more than food stamps and gave us the whole package. A year and a half later, though, "Reaganomics" cut us off. For the next three years, our sole income was my husband's part-time salary.

We experienced nonstop hardship. Every major appliance in our home died. The building we lived in was crumbling. Our children became very sick. The public health clinic became our second home.

The most we earned during that time was about $500 a month. Essentials were unaffordable. Our comfort level was measured by whether our deodorant, toothpaste, and toilet paper would last the month.

We survived and endured by the grace of God. We saw God's provision daily. It came by way of government programs, such as Women, Infants, and Children (WIC) and the Board of Health Clinic; and through caring, giving Christians. The food we ate was determined by WIC coupons and food pantries. The clothes we wore were suited to the tastes of those who wore them first. This time poverty was our choice. It was the price we were willing to pay for the sake of ministry. We saw public aid as a provision from the Lord and thanked him for it.

The people in our community don't have the luxury of making that choice. They haven't walked away from a more comfortable lifestyle for some great cause. Many of them know no other way of life. I'm always aware of that difference.

During our time of hardship, we discovered what it was like to be victimized by benevolence. I'd like to share ways this happened to me and to people I know.

The Constant Threat of Losing Aid

While we were on public aid, I would receive a letter almost weekly requiring some information or a document. These letters always included a notice in bold letters stating that failure to comply with the request would automatically cut us off from the program. It was humiliating and depressing to live with this threat always hanging over our heads. Sometimes the information was nonsensical—the thirteenth copy of information we had already provided twelve times before.

While I was on WIC, my children and I were required to have physicals every few months. Each physical included a blood test. My understanding was that if the hemoglobin count of my children's blood was normal—an indication of good health—we would be cut off. I know of women whose children were denied WIC because of their high hemoglobin count. It's a horrible thing to find yourself secretly hoping your child is not well so that you can get food to feed them.

Having to Justify Ourselves to Friends

We were the only Christians in our extended families, so our relatives didn't understand or support our choices. They didn't help us out financially or otherwise. But many times friends would call or come over to see how we were. Often they would bring food, clothes, or money. We were embarrassed when they did this; we wanted to shrink away and disappear. Yet remembering unpaid bills and bare cupboards, we would swallow our pride and accept the gifts.

After the initial embarrassment passed, we began to notice a "yucky" feeling that lingered in the pits of our stomachs after our friends left their gifts. We came to realize it came from the way the gifts were given.

The visitor's call would always start with small talk and ultimately lead to the simple question, "How are you doing?" Innocent enough on the surface, that question set in motion a routine that required my husband and me to do a song and dance before they would offer what they had come to give (although I suspect some didn't give as planned because we didn't perform to their satisfaction).

We were repeatedly required to establish need. For a bureaucratic organization, that is understandable. But our friends saw us with five little children. They knew my husband was a full-time ministerial student and working part-time. What could possibly have happened (other than winning the lottery) to move us from a place of poverty to a place of no need?

One woman described to me her similar resentment of having to prove extreme duress before she got any help. Why should fellow Christians who knew her situation require her to prove that her family was experiencing a certain degree of suffering before they would give out of their surplus to ease her burden?

One-sided Relationships

We also saw our relationships become one-sided. We were always receivers and our friends givers. While our poverty disallowed our giving back in the same way, it seemed that our friends closed the doors to our giving back in any other way. The whole arrangement was very condescending. Inferiority in the relationship was the price we had to pay for survival.

Expectations of Changed Lifestyle

We were also victimized by expectations that the gift would bring a change of behavior or lifestyle. But so much of what is available to alleviate the plight of the poor only saves them from complete ruin.

Take a family whose gas is cut off because their heating bill was so high they couldn't pay it all. People learn of this situation and give $800 to get the gas turned back on. All they've done is gotten the heat back on. They've done nothing (not that they're obligated) to change that family's ability to pay their gas bill. Yet the next winter if the family gets in the same fix, the givers often become angry. The gift brings with it an unreasonable expectation of change. People think that one act makes a bigger difference than it does.

In 1985, according to our federal government, a family of four earning $10,700 a year was considered poor. In my neighborhood, a family that earned that much would be considered rich. Five thousand dollars would be more typical. If you were to come and give a family of eight with a $5,000 income an additional $5,000, you would have blessed them tremendously. But they would still have been poor.

Those of us on the receiving end know that the help which comes our way deals with the problems of the past. It hardly touches the present—and certainly not the future.

Expectations of Changed Values

Finally we were expected to change our very ways of thinking, our values. Among unbelievers, it was outrageous that my husband and I would walk away from assured middle-class comfort for some lofty ideal.

Social workers, doctors, and social agency personnel seemed annoyed by my ability to express myself and by my grasp of the system. They would comment either directly or under their breath what a waste it was for someone with my obvious talents to accept poverty and not to choose to rise above it. I could never make them understand that was not an option for me anymore. Even our friends suggested we pursue a different ministry with a better income in a better area.

The inner city has hundreds of little churches. Most are self-supporting, which means they are poor. One pastor's wife told me how frustrated she was with people who didn't understand that God calls some from the community to stay and serve God there. She felt pressured to conform to our societal standard of upward mobility, good housing, a fine education for her children. But doing so would have forced her to move away from her own people, whom God had called her to serve. Today her family is inches from public aid, but moving is not an option God has given.

There is nothing glorious, exciting, or wonderful about poverty. If you choose a lifestyle or ministry that puts you in a situation of poverty, don't expect to find comfort in the poverty. The comfort is rather in knowing that you are doing God's will.

Poverty cannot be understood through hearing it explained. To grasp its nature, you must see and feel what it does to people. My hope is not that you will feel sorry for the poor but that you will better empathize with us, regardless of whether our poverty results from birth, circumstances, or choice.

We who are poor are also human. We have feelings. We have pride. We have concern. We have the need to be affirmed as individuals, to be recognized as valuable human beings. Like everyone else, we want good things for our families. We just can't act on those desires the way others do.

Yet on the inside, we're the same. We're all equal in God's sight. What we ask is that we treat each other with integrity and dignity, as Jesus calls us to.

Teresa Maldonado is ministering in the inner city of Chicago alongside her husband, Rafael Maldonado. Their church, Hope Christian Fellowship, is made up of community people from all walks of life.

4. Caring for Dennis

by Libby Caes

THE DAY BEFORE my thirty-sixth birthday, our foster son, whom I'll call Dennis, joined our family. On the Tuesday morning the Department of Human Services (DHS) worker brought Dennis to us, little did I know that a host of other relationships were about to enter our lives.

When Dave, my husband, and I decided to pursue foster care, we were interested in an HIV-positive child. It took several months to complete the home study and do the parent training. Only after we told the social service agency that we were ready for placement did they arbitrarily adopt a policy of not placing an HIV-positive child in a home with other children under five. Our daughter Amy had just turned three.

So we offered to take any other medically needy child appropriate for our family. We promptly got a phone call about a little boy, age two, who weighed sixteen pounds. He was still with his natural mother and desperately needed to be placed. He had been diagnosed as "dysmorphic failure to thrive." He wasn't growing and the physicians didn't know why. The social workers were quick to point out that Dennis simply was not being fed.

In a pre-placement conference, we met the hospital social worker and nurse who had been following Dennis' case. Also present were the DHS worker as well as the administrator, nurse, and social worker for the foster care agency we had been working with. Dennis, we were told, was developmentally delayed and in an early intervention program two days a week. That sounded great! I would have two days off each week, something I hadn't expected. Later that morning we met Dennis and his mom. Dennis was a charmer. Of course we said we would take him.

Five days later, Dennis was delivered to our house. A bottle and the filthy sleeper he wore were his only possessions. I immediately took him upstairs and gave him a bath. It almost seemed as though Dennis was being baptized into our family.

Later that day we learned that the social worker originally assigned to our case was being switched. Dennis's new social worker visited us the next day and did her paperwork. Then the administrator from the early intervention program called and said that one of us had to come to school with Dennis the following day to sign release papers. The DHS worker said this was nonsense, but the administrator insisted that if Dennis was going to continue his program, the papers must be signed.

When Dave arrived at the school, he was shocked to find Dennis's class made up of children with multiple handicaps, epilepsy, blindness, multiple sclerosis, Down's syndrome. What was Dennis doing there? How bad off was he?

A few weeks later, in a conference with his teacher,

we learned that although he was twenty-six months old, Dennis was functioning at the level of a nine-month-old child. We hadn't been told this before. We ourselves were just beginning to realize how far behind he really was.

Soon we discovered that the agencies involved in Dennis's care did not communicate with one another. The agency that placed Dennis in our home was concerned that we fulfill our contractual obligation to make sure his physical needs were met. The early intervention program staff were concerned that Dennis get to school and that we attend their parent training sessions. The mental health professionals wanted to continue to see Dennis once a week for therapy. The municipal human services agency was involved because it was now Dennis's legal custodian.

Two of the agencies needed to meet with us within thirty days of Dennis's placement to discuss the services they wanted to provide for him. When they wanted to schedule their meetings on the same day, we decided to make the appointments at the same time in our home. We waited until it was too late to reschedule, then told them there would be other people present. In effect we manipulated them so they would be forced to dialogue with each other about this little boy with whom they were all involved.

Although we were dealing with a total of twelve different professionals on a regular basis, there was no case manager to mediate the conflicting demands of the different agencies. The social worker from the foster agency who was supposed to do this would coordinate only the services her agency was providing. She would not interact with the early intervention, medical, and other personnel who were also involved with Dennis. We were caught in the middle of more than a few interagency squabbles.

For instance, in our orientation before becoming foster parents, we were told we could expect about twenty hours of respite a month. During this time the child would be in the care of another family. Respite care would be arranged, they said, before any child was placed with us.

Two months after Dennis arrived, we were beginning to feel overwhelmed and started to wonder when respite would start. We made a few telephone calls and found three different agencies pointing fingers at one another. Each accused the other of not providing respite services. It took more than four months for us to receive any respite.

In time, numerous other people entered our lives. They included the social worker at Dennis's school; the base service unit worker, with whom we had to negotiate respite care; Dennis's family therapist, who visited us every two weeks. Then there was the medical network. Dennis had been followed since birth by a clinic at the children's hospital. Clinic hours were every Tuesday morning by appointment. Also at the children's hospital was the WIC (Women, Infants, and Children) office, where I went monthly for food vouchers.

Sometimes we saw four different people in one week. One day it might be the social worker, who was required to visit us every two weeks. The DHS worker visited occasionally to see how Dennis was doing. Another day his teacher might visit. She came to our home monthly, and I was expected to go to the school monthly to observe. A third day the family therapist might come. The fourth day could involve a clinic visit or a trip to the WIC office. We also had to attend meetings to discuss Dennis's progress in school, in addition to the periodic reviews with Dennis's social service agency.

Of the twelve professionals we needed to interact with regularly, three were excellent—caring people who wanted to help and could listen well. The rest were just doing their jobs; they cared little about what happened so long as we didn't make waves and they could get their paperwork done. The good ones kept us going; the rest dragged us down.

A week after he arrived, I had to take Dennis to the hospital clinic. His mother had not taken care of his school physicals, so the school administrator insisted we take Dennis for a well-child visit immediately. If he didn't get one in the next week, she threatened, he couldn't attend school. It didn't take me long to discover Dennis's terror of anyone in a white coat.

Dennis received his medical care through Medicaid, and the ways we were forced to use medical personnel were idiotic. For instance, during the time Dennis was with us he had conjunctivitis and Fifths disease, apparently contracted at school. He couldn't return to school until he had a note from the doctor saying it was no longer contagious.

But the only time he could go to the clinic where he received his care was Tuesday mornings. Any other time, we were to take him to the emergency room. Should we wait until clinic hours the next Tuesday to get a note from the doctor? Or go to the emergency room sooner to see his physician, who was also on staff there?

It didn't take us long to discover that this rule was due to an economic decision made by the hospital. The Medicaid reimbursement rate for an emergency room visit is almost four times that of an office visit, thus the hospital made much more money through emergency room visits. It grated me when Dave or I would have to consider taking Dennis to the emergency room for an earache.

Early on I told Dennis's physician that I didn't want to take Dennis to the emergency room because that was a poor use of resources. She agreed that we could call her while she was in the emergency room and she would make an appointment to see Dennis in her clinic office. In this way, we were able to get around the system. It may not seem like much, but it was a small victory.

Dealing with the system became a constant battle. Some mornings the phone rang before 8:00 a.m., informing us that there was no school bus service that day. That meant two trips to Dennis's school. If Dave had the flexibility, he would drive Dennis there and could make the round trip in about forty minutes. If I went by trolley, the round trip took at least an hour and a half.

I began to ask myself if it was worth the time it took to take Dennis to school. Wouldn't it be easier to just keep him home? School was from about 9:30 to 2:30, and commuting on public transportation could easily take three hours a day. On the other hand, I was struggling with my relationship with Dennis and needed the break.

One Wednesday afternoon when Dave went to pick up Dennis at school, he learned that a short time earlier Dennis had stopped breathing for several minutes. This was something new for us, as Dennis's medical history included no record of seizures or respiratory arrest. Dave quickly called the pediatrician in the emergency room and then drove Dennis over to the hospital.

The pediatrician wanted to do an EEG immediately to check Dennis's brain wave activity, but the schedule was booked solid until after 5:00 that afternoon. Dave had an evening meeting he couldn't miss. Dennis seemed to be feeling fine and the pediatrician said he was in no danger, so Dave brought him home.

When I came to a stopping place in my peach canning, I took Amy to a neighbor's house. Dave then drove Dennis and me back to the hospital and went on to his meeting. While we waited for our appointment, Dennis's pediatrician went off duty and passed his case on to a resident. An hour later, that resident also went off duty and passed the case on to someone else. An hour after that, the chief resident decided the whole thing was nothing but a minor choking episode and sent me home. That "minor" episode turned out to be the first in a series of epileptic seizures.

The next day I talked with Dennis's social worker—number three by this time. She told me that the week before she had learned from Dennis's maternal grandmother that his mother had had seizures from infancy to her early teens. Dave called Dennis's pediatrician. An EEG was scheduled for two weeks later—too late to determine if Dennis had had a seizure or not.

At that point, I wondered if I cared anymore. I was fed up with Dennis and with the system. Life had become one battle after another—with both Dennis and his caretakers. We were constantly dealing with conflicting agendas concerning Dennis's progress.

For instance, when Dennis first came to us, he ate only pureed foods and would drink only from a bottle. He had been previously hospitalized for a month to see if he would thrive when fed regularly. He did, but when he returned home, he quickly lost the weight he had gained.

While with us, Dennis consistently gained a half pound a month. Dennis's physician was pleased; the bottom line for her was that he was gaining weight. And how did Dennis gain weight? It was simple: we fed him food he would not resist—baby cereal, bananas, yogurt, apple sauce, and a few bottles of milk a day.

But his teacher at school had a conflicting plan: she felt Dennis needed to eat textured foods. When he didn't like the textured food he was fed at school, however, he wasn't given any other choices—and would not eat. (His teacher also felt he should be beyond bottles; so he was given only cups even though he couldn't drink from them.)

I was caught in the middle. Progress according to Dennis's physician was not progress according to his teacher. Progress for me was simply getting Dennis to eat more food than he threw across the kitchen. Until Dennis could learn how to feed himself, it took me a total of at least two hours a day to feed him.

Dennis ate four times a day, with the accompanying food-throwing and horrendous messes that resulted. Our kitchen was a battleground. When he started feeding himself, the messes only got bigger. His teacher was delighted that he played with his food. (He was learning textures.) But I was the one who had to clean it up!

Yes, all children play with food. But because Dennis was so far behind, these normal phases stretched out far longer than they would have for a normal child. Diapering would also last several more years, and changing diapers was a battle as well because he did not cooperate.

When Dennis came to us at twenty-six months, he had been abused and neglected. His father was in prison for sexually abusing Dennis's older brother. His mother, who had obvious mental health problems, did not feed or change Dennis regularly and would leave him unattended for hours in a playpen. His vocabulary consisted of two syllables. He could crawl but not sit up.

A week after his third birthday, he started walking. He had developed a vocabulary of fifty or sixty words. His favorites were *Amy, apple sauce, yogurt,* and *banana.* After ten months with us, he could verbalize some needs. He loved books. Aged thirty-six months, he was functioning at the level of a fourteen-month-old.

Although he had made progress, we could see he was still far behind—and the gap between Dennis and his peers was ever-widening. Dennis could manipulate the socks off anyone, however, and that made life all the more difficult for us. Folks couldn't understand the grind Dave and I experienced with Dennis's daily care. Respite workers who came to give us a much-needed break would rave about how wonderful he was—while we fought to maintain our sanity.

By August, after ten-and-a-half months, I was exhausted. I felt I didn't care any more. Our time with Amy began when Dennis went to bed at night. But then we all got to bed late and were tired the next morning. Our whole family was living from vacation to vacation, when Dennis was not with us.

Should we give Dennis up? I struggled with the question. At first I felt guilty for even considering it. Wouldn't that only cause Dennis more deprivation and neglect? But with the help of church friends, I came to realize that we had other valid concerns as well. Our family life and personal lives were suffering neglect. Three lives were at stake besides Dennis's, including our daughter's—lives no less important than Dennis'.

We finally realized we had given Dennis all we could; we now needed to entrust him to God's care, and hopefully the care of another family. So we asked to terminate our relationship with Dennis.

That last week in August I cried a lot. This child who

had tested me to my limits, this child with whom I had a love-hate relationship, was leaving. I would never see him again.

But Dennis, it seemed, was going on to an excellent foster family situation, perhaps one even better than ours. I soon learned that his second foster mom struggled, too. I talked with her by phone several times and felt I was talking with myself.

What lessons does our experience with Dennis offer?

I was not a single mom with no access to a car. While I could not drive for medical reasons, I had a supportive husband. He could drive, had an office on the third floor of our house, and was willing to do more than his share. I was fortunate Dave had a flexible schedule. Sometimes he could take Dennis to the hospital. Then I would stay home and work in the CCHF office.

I had a church where I could stand up and ask for prayer and could meet regularly with a small group of people from whom I received encouragement. I had the support of neighborhood friends. I had an education and a strong self-image. If I, with all these resources, was exhausted after ten-and-a-half months, how could someone without these supports possibly care for a child like Dennis?

One professional we worked with told us that we were the ideal foster parents. We were doing an excellent job; we were pushing "the system"; we were advocates in the truest sense of the word. If that was true, why was it so hard? If it was so draining for us, how is an uneducated mother with several children supposed to deal with the complexities of the social service system and the multitude of conflicting demands placed on her?

If going to the WIC office or calling for respite care

was a dehumanizing experience for me, how much more would it be so for a person of color who was poor? If I couldn't make the medical system work for Dennis, how can we expect others with limited supports to make Medicaid adequately function for the benefit of themselves and their children?

Among other things, our time with Dennis taught us that "the system" can be extremely frustrating to work with; children at risk can be very difficult to care for; and without good support systems one can quickly lose heart. Understanding these problems doesn't solve any of them. But for those of us working among the poor, understanding is not a bad place to start.

Libby Caes was the conference coordinator of Christian Community Health Fellowship for six years. Currently she serves on the pastoral team at West Philadelphia Mennonite Fellowship and is in the M.Div. program at Eastern Baptist Theological Seminary.

Part II

Jesus' Response

JESUS SAID that the poor would always be with us (Matt. 26:11; Mark 14:7; John 12:8). He was right. There are many more poor people on this planet now than there were in Jesus' day (although it is likely that the percentage of the population living in poverty was much greater in Jesus' time than it is now).

We have heard the stories of just a few of the poor among us today. As Christians, how should we respond? Some of us cover our ears and refuse to hear. Others want to help but don't know how. Most of us probably feel like throwing up our hands and saying, "But what can I as one person do? How can I make a difference in the face of such poverty?"

As people of faith, we are called to follow the example of Jesus Christ (1 Cor. 11:1). Since Jesus spent almost all of his earthly ministry among the poor, we can look to him for guidance.

How did Jesus respond to the overwhelming needs around him? How did he react to the needs of the poor in his midst? Whom did he blame for their poverty? What did he tell his disciples to do?

The three chapters in this section point us to the actions and teachings of Jesus as a basis for our response to the needs of the poor among us.

5. Who Sinned?

by David Caes

> As he went along, he saw a man blind from birth. His disciples asked him, "Rabbi, who sinned, this man or his parents, that he was born blind?"
>
> "Neither this man nor his parents sinned," said Jesus, "but this happened so that the work of God might be displayed in his life." (John 9:1-3)

ONE DAY Jesus and his disciples came across a man who had been blind from birth. The disciples speculated that the man's blindness was a result of some terrible sin this man or his parents had committed. They were probably thinking about the portion of the law that refers to the sins of parents being punished to the third and fourth generation (Exod. 20:5; 34:6-7). When they couldn't figure out who had caused the man's blindness, they asked Jesus.

Jesus refused to blame the man or his parents. Rather than discussing who had caused the man's condition, Jesus spit on some dirt, rubbed it in the man's eyes, and sent him to wash in a pool. There he received his sight. When Jesus later saw the man, he offered him spiritual healing as well. Jesus did all this even though it was the Sabbath, and he knew healing on the Sabbath would embroil him in controversy.

I am struck by the difference between the disciples' response to this man and Jesus' response. All the disciples could do was stand around discussing who was to blame for the man's blindness. Jesus seemed not to care how the man had become blind; he saw the man's need as an opportunity to do the work of God. While the disciples tried to fix blame, Jesus took compassionate action.

Throughout the ages, people have tended to assume that whenever someone is suffering, surely he or she has done something to deserve it. This blame-the-victim tendency remains as pervasive today as it was then.

What is the first thing that flashes through our minds when we hear of a teenage girl who becomes pregnant? Do we blame her for being sexually active, or do we feel compassion for her and her child in their difficult situation?

How often do we blame people with AIDS for the lifestyle choices that they have made? Some Christians have gone so far as to proclaim that AIDS is God's judgment for sinful living. But if that were true, and God punished my sins in the same way, I would have AIDS too!

Our society divides people with AIDS into those with "good" AIDS and those with "bad" AIDS, reserving compassion for pediatric AIDS cases or those who contracted AIDS through blood transfusions. We haven't exhibited much compassion for those with "bad" AIDS—homosexuals and intravenous drug users.

But in God's eyes, sexual immorality is no worse than cheating on our income tax forms or manipulating the truth to suit our needs. To God, sin is sin. There are no "good" sins or "bad" sins.

As a society, we want to blame the poor for their plight. We blame them for being lazy and shiftless, for sleeping around and having lots of kids to get extra welfare. We expect them to "pull themselves up by their bootstraps," even though they lack the educational and job opportunities we enjoy.

We want to blame the homeless for their condition. "If they would only get a job!" "It's their own fault; they're alcoholics." "If he would only take a bath, maybe people could stand being around him." We want to ignore the fact that over 50 percent of the homeless suffer from mental illness.

I desperately wanted to blame our foster son Dennis's mother for his poor physical condition (see chapter 4). It took me a long time to realize she had done her best under the conditions in which she had to live.

Maybe it's just human to want to blame people for their misfortunes. Blaming is a mechanism we use to deny our responsibility. After all, if it's their own fault, why should I feel responsible to help? As long as we stand around blaming people for their condition, we won't do anything to improve their situation. Yet as long as we blame, healing will not take place. If all we can do is blame, we will never address people's spiritual needs in ways they will hear.

Jesus would have none of this. He ignored his disciples' theological smoke screens. He refused to blame people for their misfortunes. He didn't tell people their problems were their own fault. He didn't withhold healing until people confessed their sinful lifestyle choices. He didn't even make them listen to a sermonette on sin before he acted. Rather, he interrupted his plans and offered physical and spiritual healing, even though he knew his act violated social norms and would trigger opposition.

When we come across hurting people today, we face the same choice Jesus and his disciples did. Will we spend our energy debating whose fault the suffering is, trying to fix blame? Or will we see all human need as an opportunity to do God's work—and reach out in compassion to heal?

David Caes is executive director of the Christian Community Health Fellowship.

6. Who Is My Neighbor?

by Art Jones

ARE YOU a caring person?

Most of us would probably answer yes. As Christians, we are pretty good at caring—especially those of us who are Christian health or social service professionals. In our Christianity we emphasize caring for one another, forgiving one another, being kind to one another. We're clear about that.

But I think we may not be as clear about the truth that we are not called just to care for one another in our families and churches. We are also called to care for "the least of these" (Matt. 25:40, 45).

According to Jesus, taking care of people's basic needs is not an option. It is not something we do if we feel like it, at our convenience; it is something Jesus expects of us. In fact, Jesus said that where we spend eternity depends largely on this (Matthew 25:34-46).

This may seem hard to reconcile with being saved by faith rather than works (Eph. 2:8-9), but I believe that Matthew 25 and Ephesians 2 are both true. If we really have faith in Christ, the natural outworking of that is relating to the poor, ministering to their needs. It is not enough to help the affluent when they have needs. Jesus specifically says we must deal with the most needy.

"Who Is My Neighbor?"

According to Jesus, the two greatest commandments are to love the Lord your God and to love your neighbor as yourself (Matthew 22:36-40). It's not just to love those neighbors but to love them "as yourself." If I asked who your neighbor was, you might think of the person next door or somebody else pretty much like you—similar economic situation, same color skin, similar education. But when a lawyer asked Jesus, "Who is my neighbor?" that was not at all the type of neighbor Jesus described in his parable of the good Samaritan (Luke 10:25-37).

The neighbor was a hurting, helpless person

The man in Jesus' story was stripped and beaten and left half dead. He wasn't someone who had lost his lunch money and needed somebody to share a sandwich with him. He was in a desperate situation, unable to help himself. If somebody didn't help him, he would die.

A poll taken at the end of the Reagan administration asked, "Who do you think benefited most from the Reagan years?" The answers were not surprising. The overwhelming majority responded that the rich, the affluent, had benefited most from the Reagan years.

The poll then asked, "Who do you think suffered the most during the Reagan years?" Most people answered, "The poor."

Finally the poll asked, "What do you think of the

Reagan years?" The overwhelming majority of Americans approved of the Reagan record even though they recognized that the policies governing the country had benefited the rich and hurt the poor. They thought that was okay. (Maybe that's because a favorite North American Bible verse is the one that says, "God helps those who help themselves." But that's not in the Bible at all!)

Once after I gave a talk about health care and the poor, a surgeon's wife came up to me. With a red face she said, "I will have you know that my husband has a lot of bad debts because people never paid him." I happened to know where he practiced medicine; she was referring to patients who had never paid him the 20 percent not covered by insurance. She thought, therefore, that he was taking care of the poor.

But that isn't what Jesus was talking about. A lot of affluent people don't pay their bills either. Providing services to affluent deadbeats is no substitute for caring for the poor.

Who are the people in our society who have been beaten and left by the side of the road? I think of the homosexual who has contracted AIDS. I think of the person addicted to drugs and alcohol. I think of the abused woman or child. I think of the criminal in jail. I think of those in desperate situations who cannot help themselves.

The neighbor was found in a dangerous area

It was well known in Jesus' day that the road between Jerusalem and Jericho was dangerous. The area was notorious for thievery.

While I was growing up in an upper-middle-class Chicago suburb, I learned that certain areas of Chicago just weren't safe to travel in. You didn't drive there during the day without your windows up and your doors locked, let alone at night. And heaven forbid that you would think of living there with your family.

From time to time I get calls from Christian health professionals who say, "You know, I'd like to volunteer at your health center, but what about my car? Is it safe for my car?" It's as if they want me to promise them that if they come to work at our clinic, I'll make sure nothing happens to their car. What I've learned to say is, "It's safe enough for me and my wife and two daughters to live here. You decide if it's safe enough for your car."

We're pretty good at isolating ourselves. According to Matthew 25, on the judgment day the unrighteous will ask, "When did we see you hungry or thirsty or a stranger or needing clothes or sick or in prison?" I sometimes wonder if maybe they will have gone through life without seeing Jesus that way because they so isolated themselves from their neighbors. If you decide to practice medicine in an affluent Chicago suburb, you don't have to worry about the poor coming to your door. The poor have to come on the bus, and a lot of suburbs don't have—or even want—bus routes.

Not only do we isolate ourselves geographically from our neighbor; we also isolate ourselves mentally. What do we do when we get appeals in the mail from Christian relief agencies? If something about the poor comes on television that makes us uncomfortable, do we change channels, psychologically isolating ourselves from the needs of the poor?

By what criteria do we as Christian health and social service professionals decide where we are going to practice? Some of the ads I read in Christian medical journals suggest disturbing answers. Here's just one.

Why not be a better physician each year and be paid handsomely while serving the Lord? A busy practice in an economically prosperous town of 600,000. Symphonies, museums, zoos, theater, family activities, two Christian colleges, Lake Michigan, 14 state parks near by. Practice recently reviewed by management consultant and found to be in the top 10 percent of family practices nationwide in productivity. Generous salary and production income, opportunities for partnership in one year. Beautiful climate, excellent schools.

Conspicuously absent from the ad is any mention of the neighbor Christ calls us to serve. If Jesus were to write an ad for one of these journals, what might he include? I think it might sound more like this excerpt from *City of Joy*.

Calcutta had become one of the biggest urban disasters in the world—a city consumed with decay in which thousands of houses and many new buildings, sometimes ten floors high or even higher, threaten at any moment to crack and collapse. . . . Some neighborhoods looked as if they had just been bombed. . . . In the absence of an adequate garbage collection service, eighteen hundred tons of refuse accumulated daily in the streets, attracting a host of flies, mosquitoes, gnats, rats, cockroaches, and other creatures.

In the summer the proliferation of filth brought with it the risk of epidemics. Not so very long ago it was still a common occurrence for people to die of cholera, hepatitis, encephalitis, typhoid, and rabies. (Dominique Lapierre, *The City of Joy*, Warner Books, 1988, p. 31)

To want to isolate ourselves from such horrendous conditions is natural—as natural as it was for the priest and the Levite to pass by the man in the ditch. But Jesus calls us to do not what comes naturally or easily but what exhibits love to our neighbors in distress and poverty. For Christians, isolating ourselves is not the answer.

This neighbor was someone others didn't want to help

There was a reason the first two people passing by on the road to Jericho didn't want to help: it was risky. Helping the needy exposes you to risk.

You may run financial risks. Malpractice lawsuits are common among the poor, usually because of inadequate treatment and the discontinuity of care poor people often receive. I can't get an umbrella insurance policy to protect our volunteers. So when Christian physicians come to volunteer with me, they have to come with insurance they use in their own practices. As a result, several physicians have refused to volunteer at our clinic because of financial risk.

You may risk losing some of your more affluent patients. A Christian physician whom I respected highly once came up to me and said, "You know, I'm really glad you're taking care of these people. Somebody needs to do it. I tried to do it one time. When I had them in my waiting room, the kids were climbing all over the furniture and one broke my lamp. I started to get complaints from my more affluent patients. I have bank executives who sit in my waiting room who don't want to look at that."

You may even risk your life. In addition to my work at the clinic, I also do cardiology work at our local hospital, where well over 25 percent of the admissions are alcohol- or drug-related problems. That means we see a lot of patients with AIDS.

Once I was asked to put a special type of catheter in a woman who had overwhelming pneumonia. Though we didn't have an HIV test back, the epidemiologist told me she almost certainly had AIDS. As I was sticking her jugular vein trying to get the catheter in, I stuck my finger with the needle that had already drawn blood from her neck. I was reminded instantly how risky it is to take care of the poor.

Of course, you are exposed to AIDS patients when you work in more affluent areas, too. But the greater concentration of AIDS patients is being seen in the inner city and among drug addicts.

It is risky to help your neighbor.

In answer to the lawyer's question, "Who is my neighbor?" Jesus told a story that shows my neighbor is any hurting, helpless person. My neighbor may be found in a dangerous area, and my neighbor may well be someone others don't want to help.

But Jesus didn't just answer the lawyer's question. He posed a question of his own. "Which of these three do you think *acted like* a neighbor?"(emphasis added). Jesus shifted the focus of his parable from the helpless neighbor to the helping neighbor—who was not the priest or Levite but the despised Samaritan.

In this surprise ending, Jesus showed the lawyer not only who his neighbor was but how he should be a neighbor, regardless of his or his neighbor's race, creed, or religious identity. In other words, our piety or religious status does not make us a loving neighbor. Our showing mercy does.

The Cost of Being a Neighbor

It cost the Samaritan to be a neighbor to the man who fell into the hands of robbers. It cost him money, it cost him time, and it cost him personal involvement.

Being a neighbor places claims on your money

The Samaritan took the man to the inn and paid the innkeeper, saying, "Look after him . . . and when I return, I will reimburse you for any extra expense you may have."

Not only does being a neighbor cost you something; often it is impossible to calculate how much it is going to cost. Too often we are calculating with our charity. We say we will give a certain amount, but there is a limit. That is not the example of the good Samaritan. Too often the first question we ask a patient is, "What is your insurance status?" Our first examination is of the wallet rather than the patient.

My own attitude sometimes falls short on this point. At our clinic we have a sliding scale where people who are below the poverty level pay $5 per visit. I often feel good when I can take care of one of these patients in five minutes because she has a sore throat or something simple. But what is my attitude when she has eight or nine medical problems, and I have to spend an hour with her instead of five minutes—and I still collect only $5? Sometimes my attitude isn't so great. It costs us money to help the poor.

Being a neighbor places claims on your time

To help the wounded man, the Samaritan had to change his agenda. We can be sure that cleaning a robbery victim's wounds, bandaging them, and taking him to an inn wasn't on the Samaritan's "list of things to do today." To be a neighbor to the poor, sometimes I will have to change my agenda.

It's not uncommon for me to hurry into the clinic running fifteen or even thirty minutes late after being delayed at the hospital. Sometimes on my way in I see Percy. Percy has been with us a long time. He is an alcoholic who has resisted all efforts to get him involved in a rehab program. When Percy hangs around the clinic, I can be almost sure of two things. He's drunk. And the first thing he'll do is ask for money.

What is my attitude when I see Percy? Often I just ignore him and walk right by. I try to justify ignoring Percy with, "I have an agenda. I have people waiting in there who need to be seen." But the Samaritan had to change his agenda. Sometimes taking care of the poor is inconvenient.

Being a neighbor requires personal involvement

The Samaritan didn't say to the wounded man, "I'll go ahead and send an ambulance back for help." He got personally involved.

When someone comes to us with a need, do we ever give them trite answers—"Go, I wish you well; keep warm and well fed"—without doing anything about their needs (James 2:16)?

When God looked down on the world and saw what a catastrophe it was, God didn't send a check; God sent his Son. God became involved in the person of Jesus Christ to help straighten things out. As Christians, we cannot meet the needs of the poor merely by sending a check. They need our personal involvement.

Not only does being a neighbor cost your money.

Not only does it cost your time.

Not only does it cost your personal involvement.

When you have paid all these costs, it promises no immediate reward. No one patted the Samaritan on the back for all his efforts. Jesus doesn't even say the man he helped thanked him.

I have sometimes helped people who didn't appreciate what I had done, or who at least never expressed their appreciation. It's easy to wonder, "Why do I bother doing this if he or she doesn't appreciate it?"

My neighbor is not only a person who is hurting and cannot help himself or herself.

My neighbor is not only a person who may well be found in a dangerous area.

My neighbor is not only someone whom others likely won't want to help.

My neighbor may also be someone who doesn't express appreciation. Loving my neighbor costs, and it carries no guarantee of immediate reward.

While we will receive an eternal reward, even that is not to be our motivation for serving. In Matthew 25, the righteous were surprised when Christ said they had helped him. They didn't realize that when they were helping the poor, they were helping Christ, and that their reward would be eternal life. Reward had not been their motivation. In the same way, our helping the needy must be a natural outflowing of our faith, not something we do to get a reward, either now or in the future.

Excuses

If the mandate to minister to the poor is so clear, why isn't the body of Christ more involved in caring for the poor? Here are a few excuses I've heard.

It's not spiritual enough

"Caring for the poor isn't spiritual," some say. "It's the social gospel." But if that's true, why do anything except witness all the time? Somehow much of the body of Christ in this country thinks that is all we need to do—deal with spiritual needs. That's not what Jesus lived or taught.

Their problems are their own fault

We try to deny our responsibility to help by blaming the victim. Even in cases where people have contributed to their own problems, does that release us from obeying Jesus? Do we really think that coming up with excuses for not helping the poor fulfills our responsibility to God and society?

God calls us to minister to the affluent

The argument is that God calls us to preach the gospel to everyone, including the affluent. I agree. But I don't believe that excuses those so called from caring for the poor as well. That is not what Matthew 25 or Luke 10 or any other passage of Scripture says. So don't fool yourself into thinking that, because you have been called to minister to the affluent, you don't also have to care for the poor.

We have family responsibilities

A lot of people get uncomfortable and angry with my ministry choices. "How can you raise your five-year-old daughter and six-month-old daughter in that kind of environment?" they ask. Even if they don't come out and say it, I can hear them thinking, "You're not very responsible."

Christ has said that obeying him is our first responsibility. Sometimes that means sacrificing some things. Sometimes that means bringing your family into a poor community. (And I'm not so sure that's all bad.)

Many of the needy are beyond help

"If the government programs haven't been able to help them, and if all the existing private agencies haven't been able to help them, who am I to think I could do them any good?" But if we look back to Jesus' story, "my neighbor" is that person whom I can help, if only I will.

We're already helping the poor

Because we write a check once in a while to a relief agency or go to a conference on the poor, we think we are helping the poor. Let's not fool ourselves. God calls us to direct personal involvement. "Go and do likewise," says Jesus.

The lawyer's problem was not a lack of information or understanding but a lack of love. In the end, we can answer the question, "Are you a caring person?" or "Do you act like a neighbor?" not with a declaration of yes or no but only with our actions.

And Jesus will reveal how we've answered when he says to each of us, "Whatever you did—or did not do— to one of the least of these, you did it—or did not do it —to me."

Art Jones, M.D., is the medical director of Lawndale Christian Health Center in Chicago, Illinois. He lives in the North Lawndale community with his wife, Linda, and their two daughters, Kelly and Katelin.

7. Follow Me

by David Caes

> As Jesus walked beside the Sea of Galilee, he saw Simon and his brother Andrew casting a net into the lake, for they were fishermen. "Come, follow me," Jesus said, "and I will make you fishers of men." At once they left their nets and followed him. (Mark 1:16-18)

AFTER JESUS was baptized and spent forty days in the wilderness, he returned to Nazareth in Galilee. While Nazareth was an obscure little town, the province of Galilee had a notorious reputation. It was on the northern border of Palestine and regarded with contempt and suspicion by the southern Jews. Jesus thus came from doubtful origins, worlds apart from the religious and political establishment in Jerusalem.

The Jesus of Mark's Gospel is continually surrounded by poor people and social outcasts. Mark uses the term *ochlos* or "crowd" to describe the group of people who followed Jesus all over the countryside. In Greek, this is the same word used to refer to noncombatants who follow an army, performing menial tasks for the soldiers. It is clear that the people in the crowd were alienated from the leadership in the religious establishment. Mark gives several indications that the religious leaders feared the crowd.

Normally, rabbinical students seek out a teacher who can help them attain rabbinical status. This would be similar to the way would-be college students apply to a variety of schools, seeking acceptance in the most prestigious school possible. But Jesus turns this relationship around and looks for people to be his disciples. He chooses some real losers in that society—a couple of fishermen, a tax collector, a revolutionary.

Many of us have been called to work among those who are alienated social outcasts. Many of us have the education and training that could enable us to climb the social ladder, yet we have chosen to work among those our society has rejected as worthless.

When Jesus called people to follow him, he asked them to leave their economic and social security. He asked them to abandon their jobs and social responsibilities. For them, following Jesus required both a profession of faith and a reordering of social and economic relationships.

In the same way, some of us have been called to put aside lucrative or prestigious positions to follow God's call into work among those who have been rejected by society. Some of us have even had the experience of being shunned by our peers because of those we have been called to serve.

I suspect that when Jesus called Simon and Andrew, there was significant dialogue. But Mark cuts the narrative to the bone. The only words he records are, "Come, follow me, and I will make you fishers of men."

The Greek reads "fishers of *anthropos*," meaning human beings. Traditionally, this phrase, "fishers of men," has been interpreted as meaning that the disciples would be involved in evangelization—saving souls. That interpretation fits well with our cultural Christianity—all the disciples were called to do was save souls.

I do not know where that interpretation came from, but it does not fit with the rest of Scripture. The image Jesus used here comes from the prophet Jeremiah.

> "I will throw you out of this land into a land neither you nor your fathers have known, and there you will serve other gods day and night, for I will show you no favor. . . . But now I will send for many fishermen," declares the Lord, "and they will catch them. . . . They are not hidden from me, nor is their sin concealed from my eyes. I will repay them double for their wickedness and their sin, because they have defiled my land. . . ." (Jeremiah 16:13, 16-18)

The image "fisher of men" is used as a symbol of Yahweh's censure of the nation of Israel. The "fishermen" are sent out to proclaim judgment on a society that disobeyed God.

Elsewhere in the prophets, we read of the "hooking of fish."

> "I am against you, Pharaoh, king of Egypt, you great monster lying among your streams. . . . I will put hooks in your jaws and make the fish of your streams stick to your scales. I will pull you out from among your streams, with all the fish sticking to your scales. I will leave you in the desert, you and all the fish of your streams." (Ezekiel 29:3-5a)

The image of catching fish is used here as a euphemism for God's judgment on the powerful who are not living according to God's Law.

The image is also present in the prophet Amos.

> Hear this word, you cows of Bashan on Mount Samaria, you women who oppress the poor and crush the needy and say to your husbands, "Bring us some drinks!" The Sovereign Lord has sworn by his holiness: "The time will surely come when you will be taken away with hooks, the last of you with fishhooks. You will each go straight out through breaks in the wall, and you will be cast out toward Harmon," declares the Lord. (Amos 4:1-3)

Amos's prophecy is against those who are calloused to the needs of the poor around them. Fishhooks are an instrument to bring judgment on the rich who ignore those in need.

Jesus' call to his disciples to become "fishers of men" was therefore an invitation to join Jesus in his struggle to transform the existing order of power and privilege and establish a new order. In so doing, they would pass judgment on the existing order for not heeding God's call.

That judgment remains part of our calling as followers of Jesus, as "fishers of men and women." We are still to go up against a society that has channeled the poor into positions of despair.

In our work, we will grapple with a social system that marginalizes those among whom we serve. As a part of our commitment to work among the poor, we are called to bring hope. And we are called to point to another way.

David Caes is the executive director of Christian Community Health Fellowship.

Part III

Our Response

WHAT IS to be our response to the needs of the poor?

We have seen in the previous chapters how Jesus responded to human need. In the Gospel of Matthew, Jesus describes people being separated for eternal glory or eternal punishment according to how they respond to the human needs around them.

> Then the King will say to those on his right, "Come, you who are blessed by my Father; take your inheritance, the kingdom prepared for you since the creation of the world. For I was hungry and you gave me something to eat, I was thirsty and you gave me something to drink, I was a stranger and you invited me in, I needed clothes and you clothed me, I was sick and you looked after me, I was in prison and you came to visit me."
>
> Then the righteous will answer him, "Lord, when did we see you hungry and feed you, or thirsty and give you something to drink? When did we see you a stranger and invite you in, or needing clothes and clothe you? When did we see you sick or in prison and go to visit you?"
>
> The King will reply, "I tell you the truth, whatever you did for one of the least of these brothers [or sisters] of mine, you did for me." (Matt. 25:34-40)

Jesus clearly blesses those whose faith compels them to respond to the human needs of those around them. For some, caring for the poor is so much a part of their lives that they do not even realize they are doing it. For most of us North American Christians, however, it takes a deliberate effort, a reordering of the basic direction of our lives.

How do we as followers of Jesus respond to the human needs around us in the late twentieth century? What can one person do? What can the corporate church do?

The six chapters that follow contain the stories of some Christians who, having listened to the poor and to their Lord, are finding ways to serve the poor in the name of Christ. You will find stories of challenges both large and small—from relocating to a poor community to making sure that poor people feel included in your local church life. You will find some models for wholistic ministry that touches physical, emotional, and spiritual needs.

What can one person do? Only a little. What can one church do? Only a little more. What can a nation or world of churches do? Therein lies the hope of the gospel of Jesus Christ.

8. Do the Poor Feel Welcome in Your Church?

by Eddy Hall

THEIR CLOTHES are worn, their haircuts do-it-yourself jobs. Their experiences may be similar to those we heard about in the opening chapters of this book. Since yours is a middle-income congregation, you wonder, "Will this new family—*let's call them Ray and Sandra Thompson*—feel welcome?"

Your concerns are soon put to rest. Members of the Thompsons' Sunday school class go out of their way to be friendly. The family comes back. When the class has a hayride, several people personally invite the Thompsons to come along.

You are delighted when the Thompsons take their baby forward for dedication. They must be feeling at home.

Then, a couple of weeks later, they quit coming. You never see them again. What went wrong? Did they not feel welcome after all? As a matter of fact, they didn't.

This family who came and stayed awhile and left were actually friends of ours. They came to church at our invitation. My wife and I appreciated our classmates' efforts to make our friends, who were obviously poor, feel welcome. Their friendliness was genuine. But friendliness wasn't enough. To make the Thompsons feel truly welcome would have taken something more—a new way of seeing.

Our family began to learn this new way of seeing in 1979, when we returned to Oklahoma after three years away. I began working as a free-lance writer, a job that yielded high personal rewards but low irregular income. We attended the middle-class church we had attended before, where so many of our friends were, where we had felt so at home. But after attending every Sunday for a year, we still didn't feel we belonged. Why the difference between this time and last?

The difference was that now we were poor. We were of middle-class origins but now had a limited income. And as a poor family attending a middle-class church, we had run into an obstacle course of barriers—all unintentional—that kept us on the outside looking in.

Though we had attended that church for years, we had never noticed most of these barriers before. In fact, looking back we could see how we ourselves had raised similar barriers in a youth program we had directed in that very church. Only when we saw the church through the eyes of the poor did these barriers become visible.

Barrier 1:
A Price Tag on Christian Fellowship

On the evening of our Sunday school class hayride, Ray Thompson was at our house anguishing over whether to take his family. He wanted desperately to make friends, to feel a part. But the hayride would cost $4.50—and they had no milk for their three children.

We would gladly have taken them as our guests, but we had less money than they. Our family couldn't consider going.

The time to leave the church came and went; still Ray debated. He had time to drive to the farm and meet the class there, though to go now would cost a couple of dollars more for gas. In the end Ray stayed home that night and bought milk for his children. The price tag on fellowship was just too high.

The next month our Sunday school class social took place within walking distance of our home. No gas expense. Admission was just $1 for our whole family. Maybe this time we could go, be included.

But, no, it came during a time when our only regular income was $70 a week, which my wife was earning from a part-time Christmas job. During those six weeks, we had less than $15 a week to spend on groceries. On a budget that tight, one dollar was a lot. We stayed home and used the dollar for baby formula.

That was why, after a year back at our old home church, we still felt like outsiders. Though our Sunday school class had frequent socials where we could have renewed our friendships, three-fourths of them cost money for admission, child care, or both. That left us out.

Worship and Sunday school were open to everyone regardless of ability to pay. But when it came to Christian fellowship—to activities designed to promote a sense of family, of community, of belonging—those unable to pay were often excluded. For the poor to feel welcome, all aspects of church life, including fellowship, must be equally available to all.

The leaders of a women's Bible study my wife attended found creative ways to eliminate financial barriers to participation. The church provided free child care during the Bible study. Once a month, when the small groups ate lunch together, the women brought brown bag lunches rather than going to a restaurant.

To take care of the only remaining financial barrier, the $10 fee for materials, program leaders announced that scholarships were available on request. That was good as far as it went. But while it removed the financial barrier, it failed to address another barrier.

Barrier 2:
Offers of Help That Hurt

In our society, being poor carries a stigma. Even though Jesus called the poor blessed and singled out the wealthy for stern warnings, the world's valuing of the wealthy over the poor carries over into many churches. As a result, to admit to being poor, even in church, is usually humiliating. To admit you can't pay even $10 for a Bible study notebook is to feel an abasement for which few will volunteer.

To get around this, some groups eliminate fees in favor of suggested donations. This is better, but still less than ideal. When I haven't been able to give the full amount of a suggested donation, I have sometimes come away feeling guilty or even second-class. The challenge, then, is to find ways to share that don't hurt and humiliate but rather communicate love and affirm dignity.

Our present church does an excellent job of this. While expenses for this year's all-church retreat were covered on a donation basis, no one mentioned a "suggested donation." Instead, the literature mentioned the approximate cost per person but emphasized that everyone's participation was wanted. Those who could pay nothing were made to feel as welcome as those who could cover more than their own expenses. The result was that retreat participation was almost as high as Sunday morning worship attendance—and donations covered all expenses.

The exact method of sharing is not important. What is important is to find a method that allows those who cannot pay to participate on the same terms as those who can—not on a special case basis.

Barrier 3:
Practices That Say, "You Don't Belong"

Visiting a predominantly middle-income congregation is a cross-cultural (and therefore often uncomfortable) experience for a low-income family. To make the poor feel welcome, a middle-income congregation must become aware of cultural differences and adopt practices that embrace cultural diversity. Three aspects of culture—dress, architecture, and social customs— can illustrate this principle.

Dress

On the Sunday the Thompsons dedicated their baby, we were also dedicating our first child. As I dressed for church that morning, I debated. Should I wear a suit to fit in with most of the other fathers who would be standing before the congregation? Or should I wear a sport shirt in case Ray didn't have a coat and tie? I compromised; I wore a sweater.

Ray showed up without coat or tie. Sandra wore the same dress she had worn the previous six Sundays— no doubt her only Sunday dress. I could imagine how conspicuous they felt. I hoped what I was wearing made them feel a little less so. But to make them feel truly comfortable, not just one but many in the congregation would need to consciously dress *not* for success, but for comfort—the social comfort of others.

Does this mean banning coats and ties from church? Hardly. That would only make more affluent visitors feel out of place. But when visitors can look around on a Sunday morning and find both blue jeans and suits, then no matter how rich or poor they are, they won't feel conspicuous because of dress. By dressing to reflect cultural diversity, your congregation can help both the affluent and the poor feel welcome.

Architecture

What about church facilities? Can your building affect whether or not people feel welcome? Phineas Bresee, a turn-of-the-century pastor and advocate for the poor, thought so. "We want places so plain," he wrote, "that every board will say welcome to the poorest."

A middle-income congregation in Kansas City found itself a few years back in a neighborhood fast becoming low-income. They decided not to relocate but to stay and reach out to their changing neighborhood. At first, they enjoyed limited success. But when they needed new facilities, they replaced their traditional sanctuary with a "sanctinasium"—a multipurpose facility where they worshiped on Sundays and played basketball and ate potluck dinners during the week.

To their surprise, a lot more neighborhood people started coming. They felt more at home with a gymnasium than with Gothic arches and stained-glass windows. It was more a part of their culture. The building said to them, "You are welcome."

Of course, you can't change church architecture overnight. But you can, the next time your church buys, builds, rents, or remodels a building, make it a point to ask: Will the facility we're considering welcome the poor?

Social customs

Finally, how can social customs hinder fellowship?

After one of our moves, our family spent several months looking for a home church. We began attending one affluent suburban congregation shortly before the annual ladies' luncheon. Judging from the description in the bulletin and the place settings displayed in the church lobby, it was to be quite a formal affair. The price of one ticket was more than I had ever spent on a single meal. It was more, in fact, than we usually spent for our entire family to eat out.

One woman, trying to make my wife feel welcome, not only invited her to the luncheon but suggested she decorate one of the tables. This required china, crystal, and silver for ten; a round linen tablecloth; and a centerpiece. She didn't know, of course, that our "china" consisted of five mismatched plastic plates. Or that our "crystal" was plastic tumblers picked up at the dime store to get us by until we could afford to move our household goods. Her attempt to make my wife feel welcome had just the opposite effect.

The women planning the luncheon evidently had no idea that by the formal nature of the event, by their assumption that anyone attending that church would own fine dinnerware, and by the price of the tickets, they were saying this to my wife and others: "This luncheon was not planned with you in mind."

We didn't feel welcome in that church.

Putting Out the Welcome Mat

Making the poor feel welcome takes more than friendliness and good intentions. It requires learning to see through their eyes, to examine every aspect of church life through the lens of whether it tends to include or exclude them.

To learn to see this way, we will need to involve the poor in decisions that shape the life of the body. We will need to become their students, learning from them how to shape policies with cultural sensitivity.

With their help, we can find ways to remove the price tags on Christian fellowship, to avoid offers of help that hurt, and to modify cultural practices that say to the poor, "You don't belong." We can learn how to make all the body's basic ministries available to all, on the same basis, in settings where people of different cultures can feel comfortable.

As poor and nonpoor come together, not only will the poor benefit by being included and the nonpoor grow through their new relationships with these brothers and sisters. Our life together will demonstrate to the world the gospel's power to break down the walls that divide us, its power to make us one.

Eddy Hall is a freelance writer and father of four.

9. The Role of the Church in Community Development

by Wayne Gordon

THE CHURCH must do more than invite people in. It must also reach out to the local community. What then is the role of the local church in Christian community development?

To answer that question, we must begin by asking another. "What is the church?" The simplest answer is that the church is people who have put their trust in Jesus Christ and are allowing Jesus to be the Lord of their lives. The church is the body of Christ on earth. The local church is that group of people who gather together as a worshiping community, as an example of what it means to live out kingdom principles.

The traditional church, however, has often failed to live out kingdom principles. I became a Christian through a "parachurch" organization because I was not hearing the gospel in my own church. When the church has fallen short, parachurch organizations (Christian but not church-based) have arisen to fill the gap.

But there is a problem with this approach. Every parachurch organization I know of says it wants to channel people back into the church, but in reality that does not happen very often. In fact, all too often parachurch organizations actually compete with the local church for people's time, gifts, and energy. In the work of Christian community development, I think we need a new kind of parachurch organization, one closely tied to the local church.

At Lawndale Community Church in Chicago, we have created two parachurch organizations—a health center and a development corporation. Each is deeply rooted in the life of our congregation. Each helps us achieve our goal, which from the beginning has been to be a church that reaches out to people, that loves our community, that strives to meet the community's needs.

Years ago at a church meeting, we listed community needs on a chalkboard—better schools, jobs, all kinds of things. One item was affordable medical care. Once we had finished our list, I asked, "Is there anything here that we *can* do?" There was not much, but somebody said, "Well, Art Jones is in medical school. Maybe someday we could open a health clinic."

Almost ten years later, Lawndale Christian Health Center opened its doors, with Art Jones as director. Not only did the church start the clinic; it also provides the facilities for the clinic. And a majority of the members of the board of directors must be members of Lawndale Community Church. The church continues to have vital input into the clinic's direction.

Recently, during our prayer time at church, Art

stood and said that the county was planning to close a hospital that serves our neighborhood. He said we needed to go to an upcoming hearing to be advocates for the poor, to help the county officials understand that closing the hospital would hurt our community.

The county got wind that we were coming and canceled the hearing. But we went anyway—seventy-five people from Lawndale Community Church. About fifty from the hospital came too. We sat in the room and had our meeting with Art and others leading it.

The meeting room happened to be next door to the office of the Commissioner of Health for Cook County, and the commissioner sent a spy. He stood there watching us. Every now and then he would go back through the glass doors where the Commissioner of Health was, then return.

Soon the Deputy Commissioner of Health came out and sat and listened to us. The next day, Art and four or five other key people sat down with the Commissioner of Health. They began to build a plan that would make a difference.

Art could not have done that by himself. It took the church. It happened because Lawndale Community Church felt ownership of Lawndale Christian Health Center and concern for the needs of the community.

I believe the church has to be at the center of anything we call Christian community development for at least five reasons.

1. The church fulfills its biblical mission by meeting needs of community people

In the early part of this century, we saw a division between what people called the social gospel and the spiritual gospel.

But if you have the spiritual gospel without the social gospel, you do not have the gospel. And if you have the social gospel without the spiritual gospel, you do not have the gospel.

When I love my son and help him learn to read or give him food to eat, everybody says I am a great dad. But when I love the guy in the street, people say that is the social gospel.

That is baloney! The gospel is for the whole person. Proclaiming the good news of Jesus Christ means taking care of people's needs physically, mentally, and socially, as well as spiritually.

The Mosaic Law tells us that it is not God's plan for people to be poor (Deut. 15:4). But God understands human nature, so the Law continues, "If there are poor, open your hand freely to them, care for them" (v. 7). We are commanded to care for the poor (v. 11). If we don't, we are guilty of sin.

Yes, *not caring for the poor is a sin*. It is because of that sin that we have millions of people here in the United States and around the world whose needs are going unmet. And the suffering of a great many of those people is because we, the body of Christ, have not counted it as sin to not care for them.

Jesus told his followers, "You are the salt of the earth" (Matt. 5:13). The primary use of salt in Jesus' day was to prevent decay. It was rubbed into meat so the meat would not spoil. To be the salt of the earth means that we ought to be looking for places that are decaying, then going there to preserve them.

Next Jesus says, "You are the light of the world" (v. 14). What is light? Light is what comes to wipe out darkness. Where are the dark areas of our world? Those are the places we ought to be going to as people who believe in Jesus Christ.

The next time you move, I suspect you will go to a

real-estate agent and say, "Show me some nice places to live."

The agent will ask, "What are you looking for?"

You will probably say something like, "I want a place that's safe, that has good schools, something in a stable community [which probably means it's segregated], and good city services."

Do you know what you will have told the real-estate agent? That you want to live in the brightest place in that community, in the least decaying area. When you do that, you hinder your obligation as a Christian to be salt and light.

Jesus gives us two great commandments: to love God and to love our neighbor as ourselves (Matt. 22:37-38). To find out who our neighbor is, we need to study Luke 10 (see chapter 6), where the smart aleck asks Jesus, "Who is my neighbor?"

Jesus answers with the story of the Good Samaritan. My neighbor is the man beaten up on the side of the road, the person who can't help himself, the person who is hurting to the point that nobody else would even care for her.

At the beginning of his ministry, Jesus stood up in the synagogue. The scroll was handed to him, and he read from Isaiah 61:1-2.

> The Spirit of the Sovereign Lord is on me, because the Lord has anointed me to preach good news to the poor. He has sent me to bind up the brokenhearted, to proclaim freedom for the captives and release from darkness for the prisoners, to proclaim the year of the Lord's favor.

Several verses later, Isaiah proclaims, "They will rebuild the ancient ruins and restore the places long devastated; they will renew the ruined cities that have been devastated for generations" (Isa. 61:4).

The role of the church in the world is to rebuild the structures that are hurting, to raise up a new generation of Christian leadership among the poor, to repair cities or rural areas or reservations that have been so downtrodden there is only despair.

Not long ago I was having dinner with a man from India who works among the poor. In India countless people are poor. This man, though he has a Ph.D., lives among those who belong to the poorest 2 percent of the population.

I asked him, "Of all the places you've traveled throughout the world, where did you find the people to be the poorest?"

I was expecting him to say it was the people he lived among, but he said, "It seems to me that the poorest people in the world are the U.S. poor."

"What do you mean?" I asked.

"The U.S. poor are the only poor I've found who have lost hope. The poor I work with in India have hope. The poor I've seen in other parts of the world have hope."

My own experience confirms this. When I was in the Philippines, I was in an extremely poor community. Yet I saw a hope in the eyes of the squatters that I do not see in the eyes of people in my own neighborhood on the West Side of Chicago.

The church is called to bring hope. Your church may not be located in the ghetto, but it can still reach out to the poor, the widows, the orphans, the aliens, and the hurting (see chapter 12). If all our churches would be true to their calling to serve the poor, we would not need all our independent parachurch organizations. But the church is not doing its job.

2. To be wholistic, Christian community development must be church-based

We like to talk about wholistic ministry. But do we know what we are talking about when we say we want a "wholistic" approach?

Physical healing is clearly a part of wholistic ministry. Jesus helped the blind to see and the lame to walk. That is not insignificant. But even though a doctor or nurse may be able to help a patient get better, that patient will still eventually die. If all people are going to die someday, shouldn't we also help them understand what death is all about?

In the work of health care or other community ministries, it is important to link with a supportive church which can help you minister to the whole person. The church ought to care about empowering people, discipling people, enabling them to live the lives God has called them to live. When a health center is part of a church's ministry, the health center can help the church fulfill its responsibilities, and the church can help complete the healing work of the health clinic.

This is a wholistic approach. The solution to the plight of our inner cities is not simply to open a health center. Yes, many neighborhoods need one; it is a lofty goal. But a health center will not save the inner city. Nor will giving everybody a job or a nice place to live. Long-term change is going to take a wholistic approach. This means ministering not only to people's physical needs but also to their emotional, mental, economic, social, and spiritual needs.

3. A church can break down divisions between people

When health professionals work among the poor, it is not unusual for them to refer to their poor patients, those who cannot seem to help themselves, in generalities like, "they this" and "they that." In the church, however, those divisions can begin to melt. Instead of a "we/they" relationship, it can become just "we" because we're all in this together.

When those of us who minister to the poor also live and worship among those we are serving, we are no longer here to help them. We are here to work together, to help each other. It is good for both groups, for all of us. It is good for the relocated group, those with skills and abilities to share. And it is good for those who have been disenfranchised, those who did not get a piece of the pie. When we worship with each other and rub shoulders week in and week out, barriers can begin to be broken down.

4. The church is a built-in support system

If you have not been in the inner city long, you may not think you need a support system. But believe me, you cannot make it alone. You need a support system because it is tough to live in the inner city. I do not see many folks coming to live here with my wife, Ann, and me. For many years, Linda and Art Jones were the only "outside" people who had actually moved into Lawndale with us. Lots of people talk about it, but not many do it.

I once sent out a letter to a thousand people. "God," I prayed, "we are asking for just one other couple to move in and help us." I really believed somebody was going to move in. We had one nibble, a couple who said they would consider it. Eight years later, they are still not here—but they have bought a house and are trying to move in. People are not flocking to live in the inner cities.

If you sense God calling you to be a teacher, an attorney, a doctor, a nurse, a physical therapist, a dentist, a receptionist, a business manager, or a janitor in the inner city, it is not going to be easy. And if you are not church-based, I do not think you will have the support you'll need to make it.

In the past few months, I have been struggling with discouragement. It has been hard for me to keep going. I have not had the energy to do all the things I need to do. I shared that with my staff. Then I preached about discouragement one Sunday at church, among the people with whom I could share my story and struggle.

Confessing my discouragement did not automatically change things. But since then several people have called me. Others have written notes. One Sunday someone passed me a note that said, "Coach [that's what a lot of people call me], you're a good man. I'm praying for you." That was the church being the church. If we are going to succeed in the inner city, we need the church to be our support system.

5. The church keeps the various ministries in balance

Once in a while Art will be talking with someone about the health center after church. Next to Art will be the guy in charge of the development corporation and trying to run our welding business. Next to him is a person running our educational programs. Each may be needing space and resources for his or her ministry.

When we immerse ourselves in our ministries, we sometimes lose sight of what is happening around us. We can forget how our ministries relate to the whole community.

But when those ministries take place within the context of the church, the church can bring them into balance through both formal and informal channels. The church continues to bring us back to our mission of loving God and loving people, of caring for the poor, of helping people become disciples of Jesus Christ.

For the church to be all that it is called to be, it needs to be on the cutting edge of community development, finding ways to work with our neighbors to meet the needs of the community. And for community development—whether it is a health center, a jobs program, or an alternative school—to be all it should be, it needs to be rooted deeply in the local church.

If we are truly committed to bringing the whole gospel of Jesus Christ to the whole person, we will find no better way to do so than through church-based community development.

Wayne Gordon, M.Div., is the pastor of Lawndale Community Church and the president of the Christian Community Development Association. He has lived in the Lawndale community on the West Side of Chicago with his family for the last seventeen years.

10. The Church and Wholistic Ministry: A Case Study

by Glen Kehrein

WHEN Circle Urban Ministries began in 1973, our stated purpose was to minister wholistically to the residents of the Austin community, an inner-city neighborhood of 138,000 people on the West Side of Chicago.

Ten years later, the ministry had grown to about twenty staff people and four major ministry programs. By many people's standards, including mine, the ministry was a success. But was it wholistic? Were we meeting our original goals?

From the beginning we were inspired by John Perkins's vision of community development: live in the community where you serve, minister wholistically, and keep the church at the center of the ministry.

Relocation

In 1973 a group of us—including a physician, an attorney, a family counselor, and me (I had no specialized skills)—moved into the Austin neighborhood. In the sixties, blacks had been moving in and whites out at the rate of ten to twenty thousand a year. Racial tensions were running high. That was why we chose Austin. It was the kind of neighborhood which we believed needed what we wanted to offer.

Relocating into the community proved to be one of our best decisions for effective ministry. We have seen time and time again that the more removed you are from the community, the more limited you are in ministering there. A person living outside the community can do good things, but that same person living in the community can accomplish much more.

One thing we didn't realize in 1973, however, was that this principle holds true not only for individuals but also for churches. Circle Urban Ministries grew out of a church located six miles from the neighborhood. The church was mostly white, although it had an emphasis on racial reconciliation and wholistic ministry. We naively assumed that our outreach into the Austin neighborhood would bring people into Circle Church—and that would make our ministry church-centered.

It didn't. So we explored the option of networking with other churches in the neighborhood. That didn't work either. Area churches, white or black, simply did not share our vision for wholistic ministry.

In 1976, Circle Church went through a racial split. All the blacks went one direction, all the whites another, and the ministry was left orphaned. The white church, which eventually moved to a neighboring suburb, continued to support us financially. But it was no longer a church that could relate to us in a significant way.

Wholistic Ministry

Although we continued to struggle with how our ministry could be church-centered, we kept moving forward with our ministries, which we were committed to making wholistic. Our original vision was to minister by providing needed services to the community. From a storefront drop-in center started in 1974, we expanded to a health clinic, a legal-aid clinic, and a counseling center.

But over the years, we discovered that, although we could run clinics and rehabilitate housing units, one of the most important things we could do was develop people. So we started a job placement program. Before long, however, we realized that we were placing only the most employable people, people who probably would have found work anyway. We weren't really helping those who remained unemployed because they didn't really know how to work.

So we asked ourselves how we could train people to be good workers. We contracted with companies that needed hand assembly work done. The program hasn't yet taken off on the scale we had hoped, but to see even eight or ten people working there regularly is a thrilling sight. I may recognize three of the workers from the GED program, two or three from the church, some from off the street. The people running this program have created a tremendously supportive environment in which they're working with each other, holding each other accountable, challenging each other.

Since we were all doctrinally evangelical, wholistic

ministry for us also meant ministering to spiritual needs. But as antiestablishment children of the sixties, we felt that passing out tracts and cornering people in overt evangelism was insensitive and harmful. We preferred relational evangelism. "We'll act out the gospel," we said, "Demonstrate it. They'll know we are Christians by our love. People will see what we do and ask us why we do it. We'll have natural opportunities to share our faith."

The only problem was, not many people asked why we were doing what we were doing. A lot of people in Austin were so used to receiving services that they didn't wonder why we were here. They just figured it was our job; we did it because we were paid.

Despite this shortcoming, by 1983 I was feeling pretty good about what we had accomplished in ten years. We had established the ministry, we were living out our faith, we were ministering fairly wholistically to people's financial, physical, social, and emotional needs. But beneath the surface success, my evangelical conscience was growing a bit uneasy. I suspected that our approach just might be more of a one-sided "social gospel" than I cared to admit.

Achieving a Church-Centered Balance

That same year, Raleigh Washington came on the scene to establish and pastor Rock of Our Salvation Evangelical Free Church. We saw what was missing in Circle Urban Ministries: evangelism, Christian education, discipling—all the things a church traditionally does. Raleigh wanted Rock Church to provide those ministries to the same people Circle was serving in other ways.

Now Raleigh is not your typical, laid-back intellectual. Raleigh is a high-powered African-American evangelist called to preach and reach people for Christ. I didn't know at first whether to trust him to do what he was saying he'd do. It seemed too good to be true. But within a year, I was convinced he was exactly what we needed.

Now, seven years later, I've come to believe that it's practically impossible to do effective wholistic ministry apart from the church. This doesn't mean that if a parachurch organization starts a church wholistic ministry will automatically happen. It takes real work and trust to get the church and the ministry organization effectively working together.

Rock of Our Salvation Church, working in close partnership with Circle Urban Ministries, has provided a much-needed balance in our service ministry. It has broadened our vision and made it possible for us to do together that neither of us could do separately.

Some people in the neighborhood visit Rock of Our Salvation Church not knowing anything about Circle Ministries. Or they come to the clinic or the tutoring program without knowing anything about Rock Church. But once people make that first contact, we reach out to them through both the church and Circle, ministering to the needs of the whole person.

Today, if someone asks me what wholistic ministry is, I say: "Circle Urban Ministries has eighty people on staff and operates ten programs, such as housing, legal aid, medical, and education. Rock Church does the things churches normally do—worship, youth programs, Christian education. Together, that's wholistic ministry."

But I must confess another reason we in urban ministry need the church's partnership: personal support. Without it, I certainly couldn't survive. As a white person living and working in an African-American community, I experience a lot of rejection. Because of their past experiences, people in the neighborhood who know me only by the color of my skin don't trust me. They don't believe me when I say why I'm doing what I'm doing.

But within the body of believers, people trust me. They support me. If someone were to offer me a million dollars to direct an urban ministry somewhere else that lacked the support network we have here through the church, I wouldn't have to think twice before turning it down. I know I couldn't last in that environment. Without the church's support, I'd burn out.

For Circle Urban Ministries, working in close partnership with the church has made all the difference in fulfilling our original vision. After offering social services to the community during our first ten years, we finally found the missing link to wholistic ministry. As a result, no longer are we just providing services. We're seeing lives changed.

Glen Kehrein is the executive director of Circle Urban Ministries in Chicago, Illinois.

11. The First Step: A Community Needs Assessment

by Jerilyn Cochran

IMAGINE TWO CITIES of similar size with large low-income communities. Imagine two groups, Grace Ministries and Hope Ministries, made up of caring Christians from both the low-income areas and suburban churches. Both ministries are committed to "doing something" about the problems they see in the poor community. These ministries go through the typical stages of growth. One, however, invests a significant amount of energy in doing a community needs assessment. The other seems to "know" what to do.

Observation

Both Grace and Hope observe the condition of the community. They hear the "horror stories"—a young mother dies while delivering a baby alone at home. A teenager is shot in crossfire between gangs, then is paralyzed while being shuttled between hospitals. A seventy-six-year-old woman is found by her landlord weeks after dying in her sleep. Members of both ministries are concerned about what they see and hear.

Problem Identification and Organization

Both ministries are committed to action, but the members of Grace Ministries decide to find out more first. They talk with people and have informal meetings to discuss the health care needs of the community. They gather information and ask questions of community leaders and other people. They collect demographic information. A natural organization emerges as lay leaders and health care professionals begin to understand the health problems.

They identify adolescent pregnancy as a pressing problem. The adolescent pregnancy rate and resultant infant mortality rate are high for several reasons. These include inadequate information and tools to prevent pregnancy, lack of access to prenatal services, and a fear of the overcrowded local public hospital. Grace Ministries assesses its own resources and decides to respond to this problem.

Meanwhile, Hope has called local social service agencies, visited the library, and concluded the high infant mortality rate is due to a lack of prenatal services. They decide a new clinic is needed.

Planning

Grace begins to plan a program called Teens Against Adolescent Pregnancy (TAAP). Local churches offer counseling services and donate office space. The churches want to teach values as opposed to passing out contraceptives. They find out that a group a mile from them is starting a teen clinic. Teens could use the clinic if transportation were arranged.

The meetings grow as people hear of these plans. Grace participants list the available health resources and approach a local foundation for start-up funds for health promotion and transportation. They receive funding for one worker, printed materials, and a van.

Hope Ministries is also planning. They recruit a physician who will move to town when the clinic is ready to open. They are discouraged from applying as a Health Manpower Service Area, since another clinic has opened less than a mile away. They apply to a local foundation, but funds have already been committed to the other clinic. Undaunted, they slowly gather enough funds to open the clinic.

Implementation

The press loved Grace's community fair to kick off the TAAP program. The congressman came by and a local church choir sang. Reports of the event were on the evening news. TAAP in its final form now consists of 1) school visits in junior high and high schools, 2) a twenty-four-hour referral service to various health centers and physicians, 3) help in applying for insurance and public aid, 4) transportation to clinics and health care providers, and 5) coordinating hospitals allowing deliveries by residents in Grace's community.

Meanwhile, Hope opened its clinic with fairly positive responses, though they were understaffed and soon found it increasingly difficult to recruit volunteers. The demand for services was strong, primarily among public assistance patients. Reporting was burdensome, and the administration of the clinic was weak. Staff began to show signs of burnout. Patients were noncompliant, and health problems grew.

Evaluation

After two years Grace's TAAP program was thriving. A report to the funding agency showed impressive improvement in the pregnancy rate and infant mortality rate. Other local churches began to participate in the counseling and transportation. The community identified strongly with the program. The funding base expanded to include local churches that expressed an interest in health issues.

At Hope the picture was not so rosy. The physician left because he felt overburdened and confused about the poor quality of care Hope was offering. The objective health standards of the community had not changed. Eventually the clinic closed.

Why did Grace thrive? What was Hope's problem? Was it really a case of burnout? Could it be that God's hand was not in Hope's work?

Although Hope and Grace are fictional, each portion of this story has actually happened. These stories emphasize the need for a community needs assessment before developing a health ministry.

The Case for Community Assessment

When we see a need, shouldn't we try to meet it? It sounds nice, but it rarely works that way. It seems logical to want to match health care needs with the resources to meet those needs. But this "find a need and fill it" approach ignores the need for relationships and trust. Models of health care ministry should be developmental, community-owned, and action-oriented. An effective community assessment encourages such models, since problems and solutions are identified by community members, not outsiders.

In Hope's case, local people were not involved in developing the ministry. People went to the clinic out of necessity. At Grace, community members initiated the program. Trust was developed between Grace and the rest of the community. The problems of lack of trust and misdirected programs are common in health care ministries. Both problems can result from inadequate community assessment.

Traditionally, the health care relationship is one of doctor and patient—with the patient being dependent on the doctor. This model has been carried over into the organizational patterns of many health care ministries. The implication is that the doctor is the primary source of information, the problem identifier, and the solution initiator. Statistics suggest that burnout and ineffectiveness are serious problems in this model.

Many government programs, though well-meaning, have ignored individual ownership and achievement, values held dear in many poor communities. The projects have been built without understanding the communal nature and social needs of people. As a result, many projects are in shambles or have closed.

An example of this is the provision of labor and delivery services to the poor. These services have done little to reduce the factors that most heavily increase the infant mortality rate—teenage pregnancy and a lack of prenatal and nutrition services. It took the government far too many years to begin responsible prenatal and nutrition programs.

Even now, it is easier to get funding for labor and delivery services than pregnancy prevention programs. Many government programs are designed to treat symptoms rather than root problems. Some missionary activities have these same problems.

Since people's lives are involved, relationships and trust are critical. The group may have the skills or money needed to do the job, but as valuable as these assets are, the experience and support of the people in the community are even more important. An effective community assessment will identify what support is needed to determine health problems and initiate long-term solutions.

Ministries based on an effective community assessment can better avoid inaccurate identification of the problems, inappropriate solutions, and wasted efforts. An inner-city church had its heart set on starting a health clinic. In conducting its community assessment, church members discovered that the existing clinics could adequately provide the needed emergency and disease-oriented services. It still took a community-based consensus, though, to alter the church's intention to start a clinic.

The church ended up developing a health promotion ministry through local churches in cooperation with another community clinic. In the end, they saved time and resources and were able to address some of the broader health problems, including teen pregnancy and substance abuse.

Though funding should not be the only reason for doing a community assessment, most funding agencies require a document identifying problems, outlining potential solutions, and providing evidence of community support. If an assessment is conducted only as a requirement for prospective funding, the study may mistakenly focus on facts and strategies rather than the relationships that must be established.

It might also focus on solutions attractive to the foundation rather than those most appropriate to the community.

Planners conducting an assessment for a prospective funding source should not only gather the information the foundation requests. They should at the same time listen for felt needs and build the community relationships that will enable the project to succeed.

A community assessment is essential because 1) the actual need may be different from what an outside observer perceives it to be, 2) the root problem may be broader than the most obvious need, 3) the community should control the identification of problems and development of potential solutions, and 4) in doing a community assessment, resources critical to the solution are uncovered.

The Process of Community Assessment

As one facet of community development, a community assessment is conducted by a local community to 1) develop community support, 2) gauge "felt needs" and gather statistical data, and 3) identify resources that could help meet community needs (see "Needs Assessment," *NAPA Journal*, March 1980, page 30).

A community assessment takes much energy—and may take as long as two years. In some of the more effective health ministries, this assessment process took from three to four years. The required time may also be shorter, especially if the group has already done other projects.

Most people first become aware of a problem through their own observations or reports by others. Initial research needs to be done to validate those observations. Reading and talking with others familiar with the area are the best forms of initial confirmation.

The most effective way to experience a community's needs firsthand is to move into the neighborhood. No number of surveys, meetings, and research can substitute for the day-to-day experience of living in a community and seeing the problems for yourself.

Short of moving into a neighborhood, volunteering in a community agency is a useful way to begin a community assessment. Volunteer work will do little to solve the bigger problems, but the concerned worker can begin to learn about the community, its leaders, and its problems.

The volunteer can begin to identify others within the community who are concerned with the same issues. He or she can begin to understand people's attitudes and ask questions such as, "Is the community receptive to health promotion activities?" or "Have past events made the people wary about the involvement of folks from outside the community?"

Once you get to know some of the community leaders, it may be time to begin gathering for informal meetings. Try not to be the leader of these gatherings, since their purpose should be to build a team to gather information and work on the problems.

Information can be gathered in several ways. A small group can contact other organizations to find out about services already available and collect census data from the library.

Another group could develop a survey for gathering information from community members. Many people living in poor communities feel they have already seen too many studies and not enough action. Thus the wording of questions should give people an opportunity not only to share their ideas but also to express their feelings. You won't need to gather age and income information, since this is available through the national census.

A third group could begin visiting other community leaders to ask for their advice and support. This is best done by community members, not those from outside. Some community leaders may feel that the solutions are at hand and no new information is needed. Listen to their frustrations; ask what those solutions are and what is needed to make them a reality. This is the heart of community assessment.

There may be some resistance to the involvement of people from outside the community. Influential opponents to community development should be identified and included in the planning process if possible.

Other agencies should be invited to be involved in the planning stages. Local groups that can verify the study, such as the local medical society, should be contacted for a response.

The backing of leaders from all factions of the community should be obtained. For example, the New Hebron Health Center's original planning group included representatives from both the black and white communities in this small town, many local churches, and medical and pharmaceutical agencies. The result was a widely accepted community assessment, with an understanding of the potential to solve some of the health problems in the area.

While information is being gathered, other interested people can be invited to join the planning group. It is important to be sensitive to the needs of the planning group as well. What is the background of the group? What needs are emerging? What is the relationship of this group to the community? What does the group want to do most and why? Divisiveness, growing biases about community needs, or a low level of enthusiasm could indicate problems with the community assessment itself.

At this point, over a year into the process, the group should summarize results and get feedback from local leaders and community groups. Any needed additional information should be identified.

Potential solutions should be addressed. It is critical to the long-term development of the community that the ownership of the solution be with the community. The community, not the outside participants, should decide what solution to pursue. It is appropriate for outside participants to ask questions about the potential solution. But they should never attempt to "veto" the proposal. Some groups have reached an irreversible impasse at this point.

Planning for the activity that will meet the identified need can now begin. Trust has been established. The planning group can be confident that the community is involved.

A community assessment process is never complete. Continuing evaluation needs to be built into whatever project, program, or activity is initiated.

Community assessment is hard work, but failing to conduct a community assessment is time-wasting, presumptuous, and unwise. The benefits of a community assessment go far beyond the information obtained. Planners can learn from the experiences of others, build relationships critical to forming a long-term local support group, and be assured that "wisdom is found in those who take advice" (Prov. 13:10).

Jerilyn Cochran was a program officer with the Sierra Foundation. She is currently working as a consultant to several nonprofit organizations in Sacramento, California.

12. Reaching Out: One Church's Story

by James Bosscher and Carol Doornbos

HOW CAN WE as a church respond meaningfully to the social needs in our community?

To answer that question, the members of Shawnee Park Christian Reformed Church in Grand Rapids, Michigan, formed a Social Justice Committee. Our committee's assignment was to assess the needs in our community, then to select one or two areas in which our church could actively respond to need.

Four years later, our committee is about to open a short-term shelter for abused mothers and children. We have raised funds, purchased a house, and enlisted the support of six congregations. We are now forming an independent, nonprofit corporation to govern the ministry.

Ours is the experience of just one committee, but the steps we have taken in moving from research to action might prove useful to other congregations seeking to address local social needs.

1. Study the issues

The first thing our committee did was identify and study several social issues that interested committee members. Each committee member researched one issue. One studied pornography; another researched right-to-life concerns; another, earthkeeping. We knew we wouldn't be able to act on every need we found. But we hoped to identify one or two areas that would become our action issues. Here members of our congregation could actively work together for greater social justice.

2. Develop project criteria

Next the committee spelled out what characteristics we were looking for in an action project. We came up with six.

First, does the proposed action have the potential to make a significant *long-term contribution* to social justice? Or will it simply have a cosmetic or temporary effect?

Second, does the action offer the possibility for viable *spiritual involvement*? Will it provide natural opportunities for Christian witness through both deed and word?

Third, can the project be *shared*? Does the proposed action allow us to work cooperatively with other churches?

Fourth, will the project provide opportunity to *build interpersonal relationships* between those served and those serving, not just opportunity for the serving community to supply material resources?

Fifth, will the project provide *opportunities* for people with a wide variety of gifts, skills, and schedules to contribute meaningfully? Will there be a place for the lawyer, the handyman, the counselor, the seamstress, the babysitter?

Sixth, does the proposed project have *"stretch" potential?* Can it expand and grow?

While other groups might not necessarily look for the same characteristics in a project, these were important to us.

3. Identify needs and opportunities

Our study of the problems in our community revealed that some needs were already being effectively addressed. Others were not. The right-to-life movement, for example, was already well organized with strong leadership in the Grand Rapids area. A couple of churches had recently launched shelters for homeless people; thus the need for leadership in that area wasn't so urgent. We did find pressing, unmet needs in the area of domestic violence, however.

We considered several ways of approaching this need. We could work to raise community awareness of the problem. We could focus on prevention. We could operate a shelter, either long-term or short-term, for victims of domestic abuse. We could form support groups for abuse victims, or offer treatment for abusers. As we continued to learn about the needs in our community, our group was drawn more and more toward the possibility of opening a short-term shelter for abused mothers and children.

Finding answers to such questions as "Is there a real need?" and "Would we be able to work effectively within the existing social services network?" took the better part of a year. Committee members talked with hospital social workers, the Department of Social Services, several police departments, judges, and the Domestic Crisis Center (which was the only shelter for abused mothers and children in Grand Rapids).

We learned that the Domestic Crisis Center had

room for seven families and had to turn away seven to
fifteen families every month. Once assured we would
not compete with them for funds, the staff said they
would be thrilled for us to open a shelter. This would
give them a place to send those they had to turn away.

After talking to representatives of all these agencies,
we were convinced not only of the need but also that
we could count on their cooperation. Hospital social
workers, police departments, and other social service
workers would be willing to refer people to us. The
Domestic Crisis Center offered to train our volunteers.
Other churches pledged to join us in supporting such
a shelter. So far as the community was concerned, the
door for starting a short-term shelter for abused mothers and children was wide open.

4. Evaluate potential projects in light of your criteria

Our project evaluation actually took place simulta-
neously with evaluating the need and opportunity. We
were helped in this process by a social worker on our
committee who had experience working with this kind
of shelter. As we compared this possible project to our
six criteria, we concluded that it was a good match for
all of them.

It had potential for making a significant contribution
in the lives of hurting women, children, and families at
times of serious crisis.

Spiritual involvement and witness would often be
possible since overt Christian concern (deed) would
be immediately apparent. And hurting people tend to
be more receptive to the gospel (word) offered in a
thoughtful, nonthreatening way.

The project would lend itself well to the cooperation
of churches and agencies in providing funds, materials, governance, and volunteers.

Operating the shelter would require seventy-five volunteers who would take turns relieving paid staff. It would also create many other volunteer opportunities, most of which would involve personal relationships between those serving and those being served.

The project could provide service opportunities for parishioners with many kinds of gifts, skills, and interests. It would also provide opportunities for Christians from various faith communities to work together.

The project had "stretch" potential. It could expand in any of several directions—broadening the mission, serving more clients, extending care to long-term, or widening the geographic area served.

5. Seek the church's approval and support

We took our proposal to our church council first. Then it went on to a congregational meeting, where it was approved enthusiastically, with only one or two people objecting. While the church did not budget any funds for the project, they did authorize us to raise funds within the congregation.

We're not a big church, but we're a suburban church with considerable resources. Besides the presentation we made to the entire congregation, we also made presentations to three adult church-school classes. Several families gave gifts of a thousand dollars. One family, whose daughter had been abused and murdered by her husband, gave us a large gift, saying they wished the shelter could have come about sooner.

Altogether the people of our church gave gifts totaling $20,000, one-fourth of the funds needed to start the shelter. Other members provided interest-free loans.

6. Share ownership with other churches

We realized from the beginning that a project like this was too big for our church to handle alone. So we structured the ministry as a nonprofit parachurch organization. So far, six churches have agreed to support the project.

Each church has agreed to take two offerings a year for the shelter, primarily to promote awareness among their members. They've agreed to provide volunteers and participate in clothing drives. Initially, the board of directors will include representatives from each church, though that may change.

Our church's role in this process has been to start it up, then give it up. That doesn't make giving it up easy. Our committee has grown close over these years. As we get to know the people who make up the new board, it's obvious they don't have the experience in working with this project that we do. Two members from our church will serve on the board; others of us will be available for consultation during the transition.

But we're still giving up our baby, this thing we've given birth to, and it hurts. If we want it to be something bigger than us, however, we realize we have to give up control. To symbolize that this is not Shawnee's but a shared ministry, we have held off on naming the project, leaving that for the new board.

7. Get your people personally involved

For a suburban church like ours, which has been somewhat introverted, a ministry like this is a big step forward. All of the six churches, including Shawnee, has pledged to provide at least twelve volunteers, each working three to four hours each month, to relieve the staff. This will mean that many people in our church will be intersecting with human suffering and need in ways they never have before.

Though there may be wonderful moments when someone comes back to say thank you, most of the time it won't be glamorous. We're going to make mistakes. We're going to be tempted to prescribe, to give pat answers. We're going to get our noses bloodied. We may not be thanked. But that is all part of learning what selfless servanthood means.

8. Go back to step one

Four years of work for our Social Justice Committee is culminating in the launching of this shelter. Once we turn control of the shelter over to the new board, what will there be left for us to do?

Believe it or not, the committee is eager to move on to something else. Once the shelter is running on its own, it will be back to step one. Once again the committee will survey the social justice needs in our community. It will sort through potential projects in light of our project criteria and the needs and opportunities in Grand Rapids.

The process can be repeated again and again. Each time it will teach us more about how our local church can respond meaningfully to needs in our own community.

James Bosscher is a former professor of engineering at Calvin College. Carol Doornbos is a family teacher. Both are members of the Social Justice Committee of Shawnee Park Christian Reformed Church in Grand Rapids, Michigan. The shelter, named Ramoth House, opened in November 1990 and can house three women and eleven children a night. It has been filled to capacity since its opening.

13. Relocating Among the Poor

by Art and Linda Jones

WHILE ART WAS a third-year medical student, God opened our eyes to both the plight of the urban poor and the potential of ministering to their needs. Art spent six months of that third-year training at Cook County Hospital in Chicago. There he saw how inefficient, overwhelmed, and impersonal the large county hospital system was. This, he could see, was not the solution to the health care needs of poor people.

At the same time, we were becoming close friends with Anne and Wayne Gordon, who were developing a youth ministry in North Lawndale. Wayne had been substitute teaching and coaching at the local high school. Despite the advice of well-meaning Christian friends, he chose not only to work in North Lawndale but to live in this black community.

Wayne bought weight-lifting equipment and put it in his living room. The same kids he was building relationships with in the classroom and on the athletic field began to come to his home at night to lift weights. They would stay for a Bible study. As they watched Wayne live out his Christianity, they were attracted to a personal relationship with Jesus Christ.

We will never forget our first visit to North Lawndale. We were well aware that certain areas in Chicago were unsafe even to drive through. And North Lawndale was one of the most notorious. Even though it was hot and our car was not air-conditioned, we made sure our windows were all the way up.

The buildings around us were dilapidated; many were boarded up. Garbage blew past us through the streets. Many people stared at us. We questioned the Gordons' sanity as well as the potential effectiveness of ministering to people of a different culture. We did not relax again until we returned home.

Over the next months, we visited the Gordons several times. We began to meet some of the young people they were working with, several of whom were growing in their newfound faith in Jesus Christ. Unfortunately, none were plugged into a local church.

Realizing how important the local church is in Christian development, Wayne had been leading Bible studies on Christian fellowship and worship. As a result, the young people suggested that they meet together on Sunday to form their own church. Wayne had never intended to start a church or become a pastor, but the longer the group prayed, the more they sensed God's leading in that direction.

The Gordons approached us to help them start the church. Art was in the midst of a third-year surgical clerkship that demanded approximately a hundred hours of his time each week. His initial response was that starting a church was the last thing he needed. But the more we prayed about the matter, the stronger we felt God's leading in this direction. So we helped start the Lawndale Community Church in March 1978.

We had been planning to go to a foreign mission field when Art finished medical school. To pursue that goal, we spent ten weeks at a mission station in Liberia during Art's senior year. During that time we felt God's leading to work among the medically underserved of North Lawndale. When we returned to Chicago, we faced relocating into North Lawndale.

Relocation was not a decision to be made lightly. We had watched the Gordons suffer through eight break-ins into their home during the first two years of their marriage. We were particularly concerned about Linda's staying alone during Art's frequent nights on call at the hospital.

When an apartment in the Gordon's building became available, the relocation question demanded an answer. Although Art felt God's leading to move into North Lawndale at that point, Linda did not. We agreed to wait until both of us felt God's call to relocate. One year later, God moved in both of our hearts. We bought a three-flat, which we co-own with the Gordons, and we made our move.

Reasons to Relocate

The Lord has shown us several good reasons for relocating to North Lawndale.

1. Relocation provides the perspective to identify community needs properly

When you look at a community of need from the outside, it is easy to misdiagnose. The tendency is to focus on the suffering and deprivation rather than root problems. Without addressing root problems, you create dependency by removing the people's motivation to remedy their own problems. (Government programs have demonstrated this all too well.)

Hunger and poor health are real in our community, for instance, but underlying these are the problems of inadequate education, breakdown of the family, lack of job opportunities, and lack of various basic life skills.

Relocation gives us the experience to effectively plan our outreach programs. For example, as we looked for a home, we realized many of the North Lawndale residences could not provide space, temperature control, and security, we felt were important for healthy living. Our neighbors have these same needs, but in many cases such needs go unmet.

As our church plans for our new housing ministry, our experience in looking for a home in the neighborhood gives us invaluable insight. Also, as our own children become school age, we can no longer ignore the inadequacies of the local school system. Our church tutoring program supplements the school system.

Relocation has helped us understand the daily pressures unique to living in an impoverished urban area. We were obviously concerned when a man was shot in the head in front of our home—but totally shocked when it took almost fifteen minutes for help to arrive after we called the police.

Our shock turned to anger when a paddy wagon, but no ambulance, arrived. The police planned to throw the potentially dying man into the back of the paddy wagon unattended. Would our family receive the same poor care in such a critical situation?

2. Relocation helps break down racial, social, and economic barriers

The only whites who live in North Lawndale are a

handful involved in Christian ministry. We have not felt the racial pressure a black would feel in an affluent, white community. Still we were not accepted by the community for quite a while.

The most significant event in the development of our church was Labor Day weekend in 1979, when the church and the Gordon's apartment upstairs were robbed three times in two days. Everything of value was stolen. We all felt extremely vulnerable.

We met as a church on the evening of that second day to seek God's leading. Was God confirming our Christian critics who said the church and ministry would never work? As we met, we felt the power of God and a unity we had never experienced. We pressed on with a new determination and oneness.

Difficult events such as these allowed our neighbors to evaluate our commitment to the neighborhood. Idealism quickly melts in the face of adversity, but when we chose to stick it out, those to whom we had been witnessing about the power of Christ knew it was real.

Those who relocate into a poor community must expect difficult times. If they don't, they will never last. But God uses those experiences to further the kingdom and teach dependence on God.

3. Relocation provides support for co-workers

A main reason we relocated to North Lawndale was to support the Gordons. Many warned us that moving into the same building as the Gordons would destroy our friendship. Instead, it has allowed us to better support each other. We can help one another with major decisions unique to our living environment.

4. Relocation allows us to be effective role models

It is easy to criticize and say, "The problem with impoverished communities is that indigenous leaders flee with their education and skills to more affluent areas once they get the jobs that let them do so."

We agree that this is a problem. But why should we expect these indigenous leaders to stay when we of comparable skills will not move in and work side-by-side with them? Those who grow up in impoverished communities face powerful pressures to leave once they have become successful by the world's standards.

The obstetrician/gynecologist in our health center, Pamela Smith, perplexed her North Lawndale friends and neighbors. Why would she decide not only to stay and work in her old neighborhood for a fraction of what she could make elsewhere but to live here as well?

Our church has twenty-five college students. We recognize the need to raise up a new generation of black leaders in North Lawndale. We hope that most of these students will return to provide that leadership. How can we expect them to come back and live here if we are not willing to live here ourselves?

5. Relocation increases our opportunities to minister

Working in a health center in North Lawndale has given Art many chances to build relationships with people and share his faith. Our life outside the clinic provides additional opportunities for witnessing among people we would not see at the health center.

This allows Art to build relationships based on common interests or needs rather than on a physician-patient relationship and resultant role expectations. For example, Art is building good friendships with people he meets when he takes our five-year-old on bike rides around the neighborhood. These friendships translate into opportunities to witness for Christ.

6. Relocation enhances credibility
with funding sources

Obviously, you should never relocate into a poor community solely to improve the prospects of funding a program. However, as we look back on God's provision for ministry in North Lawndale, we see the importance our relocation has played in attracting funding for the clinic and other ministries.

Relocation communicates to the funding source how serious and important your work is for you. It sets you apart from the myriad of other applicants vying for scarce foundation and charity dollars.

7. Relocation enables us to obey God's Word

The most important reason to relocate among the poor is to obey God's Word. Numerous Scriptures, such as Matthew 25, make it clear that caring for the poor is not optional in God's eyes. Although God does not require us all to relocate to follow this command, God does direct many of us to do so. It is difficult for us to look at the geographic distribution of Christian health professionals and not wonder if some of them are missing out on God's best for their lives.

Maintaining Your Relocation

You don't have to visit too many ministries among the poor to fill a book with examples of burnout. Too often, ministry among the poor is like being a youth pastor. You start out full of enthusiasm, work intensely, tire, and then move on in life.

This "peace corps" mentality takes its toll on Christ's ministry in a poor community. People in the neighborhood become reluctant to open up and develop a friendship with the newest staff member; they realize it will probably be a transient friendship. We feel a long-term call to working in North Lawndale and are taking the following steps to make this practical.

1. Pace yourself

It is easy to become so overwhelmed by the needs around you that you try to push beyond your capacities. People often come to Art with physical complaints that are symptoms of nonmedical stresses in their life. You will become very frustrated if you try to be physician, social worker, nutritionist, pastoral counselor, and legal adviser all at once.

Whatever your career, define your skills. Then find others with whom to network; they can help meet needs you are not best qualified to address. For a physician, this would mean limiting after-hour work to true emergencies. Remember that God has given you responsibilities with family and friends as well.

2. Build a support group of like-minded friends both inside and outside the community

One of the best support groups Linda has is a group of women involved in Christian ministries among the poor in other Chicago communities. (It is amazing how therapeutic a session on dealing with cockroaches can be!) Don't be afraid to discuss your feelings of frustration and doubt as well as your triumphs.

3. Escape from the neighborhood at least once a month

It can be difficult to guard family time and easy to lose perspective when working in an impoverished urban community. We have partial ownership of a small cottage on Lake Michigan, located just outside of beeper range an hour and a half from home. Even if only for twenty-four hours, we try to get to the cottage once a month. Here our daughters can run around and have some sense of independence. We find this refuge essential to maintaining our perspective, our walk with the Lord, and our long-term effectiveness.

4. Expect criticism

Your relocation will bring you criticism. It will make some Christians uncomfortable with their own affluent lifestyle—and maybe their previous refusal to heed a similar call from God.

Often the criticisms will be subtle. They may come in the form of seemingly honest questions like, "Isn't it difficult to raise your child in that environment?" But we know that what most questioners are really saying is that responsible parents would never drag their child into such a situation. Criticism can be devastating if not expected and understood.

5. Don't judge your success by the world's standards

Outsiders, especially funding sources, will try to impose their standards of success. Systematically evaluate your work to improve its effectiveness, but don't yield to others' demands for instant success. God calls us to be faithful. Our success is how well we do that, not some arbitrary numerical evaluation.

There are tremendous opportunities to serve God among the poor. Despite its difficulties and temporary hardships, relocating to your neighborhood of ministry in obedience to God can only enhance your effectiveness among those to whom God has called you.

Art and Linda Jones have lived in the North Lawndale community of Chicago, Illinois, for twelve years. They have two daughters, Kelly and Katelin. Art is the medical director of the Lawndale Christian Health Center.

Part IV

Overcoming Obstacles

IT IS EASY to romanticize those living or working among the poor. We are impressed by their commitment to God and to their work. And we may be tempted, in our admiration and our inspiration to try to be like them, to overlook the struggles involved in working among the poor.

Those who live and work among the poor have to face the same problems the poor themselves struggle with daily. These include crime and violence, dirty streets, substandard housing, lousy schools, inadequate city services. Being a middle-class Christian who wants to serve God among the poor doesn't make you immune to break-ins!

The work is hard, just as in any place where the resources are inadequate. Sometimes it is unrewarding. Often it is tiring.

God understands how difficult it can be. Even Jesus got tired and withdrew from the needy people around him (Mark 4:35-38). Once Jesus was so exhausted from his work that he slept through a storm that threatened to capsize the boat he was in (Mark 4:35-38; Luke 8:22-25). Maybe Jesus knew what we modern-day Christians are just beginning to acknowledge. We must take care of our own as well as others' needs or we will quickly "burn out" and be of little use to anyone.

Ongoing stress, cross-cultural misunderstandings, discouragement, and feelings of failure are among common obstacles Christians face in serving among the poor. Jesus never promised that obedience to him would be easy. Many give up. In the remaining chapters of this book, those who haven't given up identify obstacles they have faced in their work. They reflect on how they have made it through by perseverance, the encouragement of fellow Christians, and God's grace.

They have counted the cost—and have been willing to pay the price. As we listen to the poor, so must we listen to those who have served in their midst.

14. Caught Between Two Worlds: Managing Stress

by Brent Lindquist

FOR THE LAST thirteen years, I have worked with missionaries from almost every continent of the world. My role has been to build them up, train them, send them off, and help restore them when they come back bruised and hurting.

These missionaries are working in foreign countries. However, those working in health or social service ministries here in the United States also struggle with many of the same issues of stress, particularly if their ministries are in cross-cultural contexts.

Caught Between Two Worlds

I work in two worlds. I am a Christian who happens to be a psychologist. In the world of psychology I am the competent, autonomous health care provider helping people deal with their various emotional, familial, and personal difficulties. Yet some of my psychologist friends wonder about me—do I take that Christian stuff too seriously? Some of my Christian friends wonder about me, too—have I been perverted by all that psychology stuff? Many Christians who don't even know me judge me harshly on the grounds that I use psychology in my work.

We all deal to some extent with this question of how to gain trust from the various populations in which we work. Perhaps your faith has led you to work in a particular community, but your Christian colleagues or supporters question whether your social activism is a sign of creeping liberalism. On the other hand, some of the people with whom you work are just as concerned about the needs of the community as you are. But they have no faith to motivate their actions and wonder if you are some sort of religious fanatic.

It is difficult to build trust in either circumstance. It is hard to work in a world with gray tones, particularly when the people with whom you associate see only black or white.

Confused About Feelings

I am not known as a Bible-thumping psychologist. I don't glibly use Scripture verses to soothe over a person's pain. I will let a burned-out missionary rant and rave in anger at God or express frustration at a Bible that seems meaningless. If that is a person's feeling, I certainly don't want to heap on more expectations or guilt.

Several years ago I was working with a missionary who had had a painful experience in her mission field. That experience brought out some things from her past that made her even more miserable. One day she told the other members of her women's group that her therapist had taught her more about God than she had learned in most other places. This was an interesting comment coming from a seminary graduate.

Questioned further, she said she was able to be honest with me. She could be angry, hurtful, hateful, and bitter—yet she never felt rejected by me. She added, "If he can be that accepting of me, how much more can the Lord be accepting of me and my feelings?"

My point is not to persuade you that I am a good therapist. Rather, I tell this story to raise fundamental Christian questions. Is it okay to be honest about how you are feeling? Is it okay to admit to somebody that what you do in your health ministry or your community development project is hard? Is it okay to tell people that you question whether you are really making an impact on people and that sometimes you feel like giving up?

The answer I hear coming from some Christians is, "No, it is not okay to be honest. Our supporters don't like to hear that." Indeed, many missionaries tell me that if they were honest about what they were going through, within a few months they would lose all their support. I have noticed that the people who pull through most easily are those who tell me they have supporters with whom they can be honest.

It is critical for each of us to have people with whom we can be honest, no matter how badly things are going. Do you have people with whom you can be honest about what you are going through? If you do, wonderful. Don't stop being honest. If not, begin immediately to pray for and seek out such a person.

Finding Hidden Sources of Stress

Many missionaries come to me saying they are stressed by their work and the culture they work in. It may be true that their jobs are stressful. It is true that every culture has stressful components, and that these cause difficulties.

But often the root causes of their stress are to be found not in their work but in unfinished business left over from childhood. The job and the unfamiliar culture only bring these problems to the surface. It is crucial to identify the true sources of our stress.

Many events in our lives can produce problems for us well after they happen. Child abuse, sexual abuse, and alcoholic families can cause lifelong difficulties. Such problems don't always get completely taken care of when we turn our lives over to Jesus. He is our Lord, but sometimes we don't allow him to be Lord over everything. Often we are not even aware of some of these things until stressful conditions bring them to the surface.

Cross-cultural ministry may force us to face the question, "What is the source of our stress?" If it is coming from our job, that calls for one kind of response. But if it is coming from past events in our lives, that calls for dealing directly with those events and their consequences—which may not be easy.

Identifying Expectations

Expectations for our ministries can be grand steps of faith or real killers. We all have expectations of ourselves in relation to our ministries. Many of us also have to deal with expectations developed by the boards under which we are working. Sometimes supporters unknowingly put destructive expectations on us which can cause stress and burnout. And the people we are trying to serve also have expectations of us.

In dealing with the stress that all these expectations can cause, it is important to identify where each of your expectations is coming from. List all expectations you must work with and look at them realistically. Can you accomplish them? Do you need help? Do you need additional resources?

You may think certain expectations are coming from the community in which you are working—when in fact they are not. Have you ever asked the people you work with what their expectations are? You may think they want a health clinic, when what they may really want is someone they can talk to.

This raises the question of whose ministry it really is. Is this ministry one that you and the Lord have worked out with the people you are serving. Or has it been forced on you by the congregation that supports your work?

Managing Stress

Each of us seeking to alleviate some of the stress in ministry must wrestle with four big issues identified below. It is not an easy task. Some answers may cause you further pain, while others may lead you out of pain.

- Do you have people with whom you can be honest?
- What are the roots of your stress?
- Are you working with unrealistic expectations?
- Whose ministry are you trying to accomplish?

Look at these questions. Then begin a regular period of self-analysis and reflection accompanied by Bible study and prayer. Seek the guidance of people with whom you can be accountable. Taking these steps will help you keep balance in your life and give you the strength to effectively manage your stress.

Brent Lindquist, Ph.D., is president of Link Care Center in Fresno, California. He serves as consultant to almost one hundred mission boards (where he is known as "the shrink from Link"), coordinates pre-field and field programs, and counsels missionaries undergoing a wide variety of struggles.

15. The Dividing Wall of Hostility: Crossing Cultural Lines

by Dawn Swaby-Ellis

A COMMITTED, God-fearing doctor who is white was once telling me of his frustration with his patients. Though he has worked with the predominantly black population of a large inner-city hospital in Atlanta for thirty years, he still can't understand them.

"They just make no sense to me," he complained. "They break every taboo; they're noncompliant; they don't care about their children. And where are the black men? Do they exist, or are they just shadows that slip in and out of houses at night?"

He went on to describe the work of an anthropologist at a local university who had studied a particular African tribe. "This tribe had very clear traditions about when to start intercourse and relationships with the opposite sex. Sexual practices were closely supervised," he said.

"And they mirrored to a large extent the values I gained from my own small-town upbringing," he went on. "But there is no comparison between this tribe and the people we have here. They're just completely licentious. In one U.S. city, the mean age for black males to start intercourse is 11.8 years. This means the range is from ages 8 to 14."

He looked at me squarely and asked, "Do you know that crosses every taboo in my mind? Who are these people anyway?"

I answered as calmly as I could. "Well, there are some differences between that African tribe and that child you are treating in the emergency room. The differences were caused by three hundred years and an experience called slavery."

"What does that have to do with it?" he asked.

I swallowed hard. Before me stood an intelligent, well-read man who had lived through the sixties and the civil-rights era. He had heard many speeches about the plight of blacks in America. I thought he would have known what the ravages of slavery did to a people.

I thought that, faced with such questions as why young boys have intercourse and why black men fail to shoulder the responsibility of their families, a well-educated doctor would be able to trace some of these problems. He should be able to see the wounds caused by separation from tribe and family on the slave ships and plantations.

I thought he would know that if a young slave was caught visiting his fiancée on another plantation, the consequences to him—and to her in front of him—are not fit to be retold.

I thought educated North Americans knew the history of slavery and its consequences. I was painfully wrong.

When I mentioned this conversation to a Christian colleague, she told me, "No, Dawn, that isn't surprising. A lot of people don't know those things, particularly here in the South."

That's when I first realized the importance of talking specifically about how to handle our cultural, ethnic, and class differences in service among the poor. I used to think this was unnecessary, especially among Christians. After all, we Christians are all one in the Spirit. And we know that God created each of us. So it really doesn't matter what color we are or what culture we're from, right?

Wrong. It's not unusual for Christians of different cultures not to know about each other's backgrounds, even right here in North America. We eat each other's food and wear each other's clothing styles. But we don't know each other on an individual, personal level. If we're going to learn how to serve each other as health care or social service professionals, it will take more than a passing handshake or a dinner at a Chinese restaurant.

I once visited a friend in Philadelphia who lived in a middle-class half-black, half-Jewish neighborhood. One day we had some Jewish children and some black children over to play.

A black child from the apartment building burst into the room where everyone was playing happily, took one look around, and announced, "I don't want to stay here. I don't want to play with them. They be white kids!"

My friend responded, "They are our friends. So you just sit down right there and play with them." Before long, they were all playing together just fine.

Ethnic attitudes—negative and positive—are both taught and learned, beginning at an early age. Though that means they are deeply ingrained, it also means we can relearn them. When we serve among the poor, we must work at conquering the ethnic, cultural, and class barriers we have all learned.

For instance, a group of medical students working in an ethnically homogeneous area in Jamaica were mostly middle class, while their patients were from the working class. The hospital social worker and I saw that we needed to organize a home visitation program for the students so they could understand why some of the treatments they were prescribing wouldn't work.

You couldn't tell a mother to go home and mix powdered milk with cold water, for instance, when she had no refrigerator and had to walk a mile for water. If you don't know your patients' living conditions, your instructions will set them up for noncompliance.

Such ministry problems are due to a combination of racial, ethnic, and economic differences. They can occur wherever one person is insensitive to the values and life situation of another. Studying cultural and ethnic backgrounds is therefore important to the work of health care professionals or others desiring to live out God's call among the poor. This leads us to obeying an important aspect of God's call—cross-cultural reconciliation. Paul writes,

> For [Christ] himself is our peace, who has made the two one and has destroyed the barrier, the dividing wall of hostility, by abolishing in his flesh the law with its commandments and regulations. His purpose was to create in himself one new man out of the two, thus making peace, and in this one body to reconcile both of them to God through the cross, by which he put to death their hostility. (Eph. 2:14-16)

We know God calls us to cross-cultural relationships

because of Jesus' death on the cross, which destroyed the divisions and barriers between us. This doesn't mean we lose our own identities. Instead, God calls us to unity in the midst of our diversity.

How can God's provision for this unity become a reality in our experience? I believe it involves a process. We need to commit ourselves to this process whenever we prepare to practice in a new culture, even in our own country. Here are important steps.

1. Read widely about the other culture

When I came to this country from Jamaica and married my African-American husband, I thought, "I'm black. I share a common slave/colonial heritage. I know all about my husband's background."

But my husband challenged me to stop talking about what it meant to be black in the United States until I had read more about the African-American culture. (*Black* and *African-American* are synonymous terms currently used for people brought to the United States from Africa in slavery. They represent tribes of various origins and varying degrees of interracial admixture.)

My husband put a stack of books on my desk, including *The Invisible Man* by Ralph Ellison and *From Slavery to Freedom* by John Hope Franklin. Six months later, after reading all those books, I was beginning to talk about the American black experience with more understanding.

And I began to sound more authentic to my husband, who had gone through much the same process in learning to understand my African Caribbean culture. We could then begin a more sensitive dialogue on the condition of our respective peoples.

2. Befriend someone of another culture

I believe it's important to choose to fellowship with someone of a different ethnic group, knowing full well that it won't always be easy. A lot of mistrust exists between the ethnic groups in this country; often people feel that efforts at such friendships are not genuine.

Trying to build an authentic cross-cultural relationship will involve risk and pain. Sometimes you may be rejected. Finding and developing a solid relationship will require persistent, ongoing fellowship—and your only reward may be that in the end you are found trustworthy.

3. Pray for a spirit of communication and understanding

Years ago in Jamaica I heard evangelist Tom Skinner interpret the wind and fire and tongues of Pentecost. The wind, he said, was the symbol of regeneration. The fire symbolized purification. And the tongues were a gift of communication—the ability to communicate with those of other nations and cultures.

When I heard that, I thought, *That is still what the Holy Spirit wants to do in us. God's Spirit can give us a spirit of communication that enables us to hear and be heard across ethno-cultural barriers.*

4. Pray that God will continue to crucify the "old person" in us

Who we are is defined by the schools we attend, the clothes we wear, the family we belong to, the career we have, our position in the community, whether we belong to a minority or majority ethnic group. We hold dear our privacy, our dignity, our achievements, our families, our homes, our heritage, our country. All these, too, help define who we are.

But the established norms of our culture we hold dear may not be the values God holds dear. As we hold our values up under God's light, we may find that what we once held sacred is no longer to be important to us.

Do you remember Peter and Paul in Antioch? Peter wasn't doing well in his cross-cultural relationships with Gentiles

> Before certain men came from James, he used to eat with the Gentiles. But when they arrived, he began to draw back and separate himself from the Gentiles because he was afraid of those who belonged to the circumcision group. . . . When [Paul saw he] was not acting in line with the truth of the gospel, [he] said to Peter . . . "You are a Jew, yet you live like a Gentile and not like a Jew. How is it, then, that you force Gentiles to follow Jewish customs?" (Gal. 2:12, 14)

Whatever ethno-cultural value we hold dear that proves divisive in our relating to those of another culture—that is what we are asked to give up.

Paul goes on, "We who are Jews by birth and not 'Gentile sinners' know that a [person] is not justified by observing the law." We are not justified by holding onto that custom or value that we hold dear. No, we are "justified by faith in Christ" (Gal. 2:15-16a).

Developing an authentic cross-cultural relationship requires a dying to self, which includes dying to our ethno-cultural values and identity. We won't automatically experience the unity Christ has provided for us through his death. It will take work for us, just as it did for the first disciples.

To experience Christ's unity with those of other cultures, classes, and ethnicities, we will need to commit time and effort to study. We will need intentionally to develop cross-cultural personal relationships. We will need to ask the Holy Spirit for a spirit of communication, the ability to hear and be heard across ethno-cultural barriers. And we will have to die to self, to give up any ethno-cultural values and customs that prove divisive—values that may be as important to our identity as circumcision was to Peter's sense of who he was.

Cooperation with God's transforming work in our lives will help our attempts to serve the poor across ethnic, cultural, and class lines move. Such cooperation will help us move beyond paternalism to sensitive, authentic servanthood.

Dawn Swaby-Ellis, M.D., is a pediatrician working in Atlanta, Georgia.

16. A Path Toward Healing: Dealing with Discouragement

by Katie Pitkin

"Why are you so downcast, O my soul? Why so disturbed within me? Put your hope in God, for I will yet praise him, my Savior and my God." (Ps. 42:5-6)

FOR ME, discouragement came as a surprise.

After positive cross-cultural experiences with *campesinos* (farmers) in Central America and migrant farm workers in the United States, I was convinced God had called me to serve in Latin America. I first went to Ecuador with the Fulbright Commission on a one-year grant for independent research in public health. I planned to study nutrition at the Technical University of Chimborazo and do rural fieldwork in maternal-child health.

Shortly after arriving in Ecuador, I connected with the staff of MAP International, a Christian organization working in community health development. MAP put me in touch with a Quichua woman named Maria, who was trying to develop a women's health program for local Indians.

Maria had recently begun teaching health as part of a series of week-long "Bible Institutes" for women sponsored by the Association of Evangelical Indians of Chimborazo (AIECH). When she asked me to help, I eagerly agreed. I was excited about what I perceived to be a wholistic approach to health that integrated biblical teaching and health. Maria seemed pleased to have a helper.

Racism

My daily activities included planning and conducting workshops with Maria, studying Quichua, and going to classes at the university. Working alongside Maria, I began to witness the pain of racism. The *mestizos* (people of mixed Spanish and Indian parentage) openly discriminate against the Quichua Indians.

Although I was not a direct victim of racism, my new friends experienced the dehumanizing treatment daily. I felt torn apart inside when I saw others treat Maria as if she did not deserve their time or respect. Many people thought I was crazy to be working with the Quichua.

In Chimborazo, racism penetrates all aspects of daily living—the bus, the market, public offices, and even church. I had hoped to find a different attitude among Christians. Instead I found many of the same racist attitudes, along with a self-righteousness that created further divisions.

I became discouraged with my living situation because my landlord would not let me have Indian visitors into my home. I wanted to live with a Quichua family, but at that time there wasn't an opportunity to do so. When I went to Maria with tears of frustration, she took me to the home of a woman she knew from church. The woman offered me a room and assured me I could invite anyone to the house. "We are all God's children," she said.

Once I moved in, however, the family would forbid any Quichua friends I had over to enter certain parts of the house. The family treated my friends with contempt, and made derogatory comments about those they considered less than human. Perhaps because I hoped to be a bridge of reconciliation, I stayed with this family for four months. But my daily encounters with dividing walls of hostility in both the house and the town brought frustration and discouragement.

In my anger, I let walls build between myself and those who took part in this dehumanization. I had little patience with those who criticized the Indians as being dirty and stupid or accused them of being thieves. I was especially impatient when I saw such people taking advantage of the Indians.

When communication felt too difficult, I often withdrew. I sought comfort in the Psalms and reflected on the meaning of reconciliation. I saw how we often talk about reconciliation between God and ourselves—but hesitate to deal with reconciliation with our own families, friends, and acquaintances. Many of us are quick to denounce apartheid in South Africa, but we fail even to acknowledge racism in the United States.

Loneliness

In my search for friends, I felt I was encountering only impenetrable walls. The question that seemed to follow each introduction was a wary, *"De que religión eres tú?"* ("What is your religion?") Trying to explain that I did not follow a religion but desired to follow Christ only hindered further communication. I sought to understand the historical and contextual reasons for this distrust while struggling with feeling alienated from those around me.

I longed for kindred spirits with whom I could work through these issues. I received moral support from the MAP staff. But they lived in Quito or other provinces and were involved in other programs, too far away to meet my need for community.

Lack of Results

As a Fulbright Scholar, I felt responsible to produce something noteworthy, yet my first year stirred more questions than answers. My studies at the university proved to be mostly a waste of time. I saw no tangible results from my work with the Quichua women. Progress with the Bible Institutes was slow, partly because the women weren't clear whether they wanted a traditional Bible-training program or a more integrated program including health, nutrition, and food preparation. We often seemed to be spinning our wheels.

Because I was not achieving my goals, I began feeling I had totally failed in my work with the Indians. I became increasingly frustrated with myself. This sense of failure only added to my discouragement.

Disillusionment

My experience also raised serious questions for me about the mission of the church, the purpose of development, and my role as an expatriate. I found myself in disagreement with much of what had been done by missionaries in Ecuador, as I felt that the gospel had become disturbingly North American.

The dichotomization of life into "spiritual" and "material" realms seemed even more inappropriate in this cultural context than in North America. I grew tired of seeing the same old methods of evangelization and church organization translated into Spanish or Quichua, then plopped down without regard to their appropriateness in that culture.

I also became discouraged at what I saw being done in the name of community development. Some outsiders waving the banner of community development brought paternalistic attitudes and handout programs that did little to develop the community. They came to "help" and worked from the premise that the Indians "needed" them. They thought they had all the solutions to the Indians' problems. Although they espoused community participation, they retained control over *their* programs because they saw themselves as the community development experts.

The more I struggled with these issues, the more convicted I became of my own pride and paternalistic attitudes. At times I caught myself sounding pharisaic. I knew I needed to change—yet the prospect of making those changes seemed overwhelming.

I was also discouraged by the infighting and dishonesty among the Indians themselves, which seemed to hurt their cause and hinder the development process. Father Albert Nolan describes this phenomenon in his article, "Four Stages of Spiritual Growth in Helping the Poor."

The fourth and last stage of development begins with the crisis of disillusionment and disappointment with the poor. It begins with the discovery that many poor and oppressed people have faults, do commit sins, do make mistakes, do fail us and let us down or rather fail themselves and sometimes spoil their own cause. (*Health and Development*, Winter 1987, p. 11)

I saw greed, jealousy, selfishness, and the desire for power cause divisions and misunderstandings in the Indians' own organizations. It made me question whether I could continue to participate with integrity. This was particularly the case when I saw Maria succumb to those power games herself, then learned she had accused me of being unfaithful to her.

After this attack, I entered a "dark night of the soul." I began to question whether the many years of exploitation and manipulation by outsiders meant that the Quichua would never fully trust anyone from outside again. I despised being on the outside and longed for deeper relationships built on genuine trust.

Spiritual Dryness

Unlike other times of testing, when I have been drawn to reading Scripture, prayer, and reflection, I passed through a spiritually dry time, a desert experience. My lack of desire to read Scripture and pray brought only more feelings of guilt.

I tried to find encouragement in familiar passages that had helped me in the past, but they did not comfort me now—and that only deepened my guilt. I began to doubt my spirituality and wondered if I had been deceiving myself for all these years. The fire inside had begun to dim. I was not sure if I could fan the flame, or if it would soon go out.

Personal health problems further complicated matters. A painful foot problem hindered my walking, and a continuous battle against intestinal parasites made me feel miserable. Neither problem required hospitalization, but they kept me down because they seemed to have no remedies.

I felt handicapped. Feelings of guilt continued to plague me. "Katie," I'd tell myself, "you shouldn't let these problems bother you. Some people suffer from much worse things—and you're complaining about this?"

The racism, my disillusionment with missions and development programs, the lack of results in my work, and my isolation and loneliess—all contributed to my discouragement. I wondered if I should continue with my work and doubted I could ever be happy in it.

The Beginning of Healing

After two and a half years, I am still in Ecuador—and enjoying my work. What happened?

The healing process has been a long one and continues to this day. Most important in the process was allowing myself to *feel* all my feelings of discouragement, disappointment, hurt, and anger. I can identify with F. Scott Peck, who says of his growing-up years: "Whenever I was anxious, I became anxious about being anxious. Whenever I felt depressed, I got more depressed over being depressed."(*A Different Drum*, Simon and Schuster, 1987, p. 28)

Because I did not want to cover my wounds with a false sense of well-being and a shallow spirituality, I tried to work through my feelings in a spirit of self-acceptance. My perfectionism made this hard. If I cannot "produce" perfectly in my work and in relationships, I expect I should at least always *respond* in "the right way" to my circumstances. That expectation leaves little room for discouragement, anger, and disappointment.

This is one reason my experiences with discouragement were so devastating to my spirit. I felt guilty for feeling discouraged. I felt guilty that such human struggles as physical difficulties and a need for deep friendships had gotten me down. And I felt guilty that I had not found consolation in the spiritual disciplines of prayer, study of the Word, and meditation.

Affirming Humanness

Ironically, it was in this struggle with my humanness that I began to experience healing and growth. A long-time friend and mentor told me that it seemed like my first year had been one of affirming my humanity. That put my discouragements, struggles, and disappointments in a positive light. It helped me understand what it means to be a human as well as a spiritual being.

As I grew to appreciate *all* the different aspects of my being, I began to discover beauty and creativity in both humanity and spirituality. My goal became to integrate and balance these different aspects rather than focus only on becoming more spiritual.

Becoming a Student

Not all of my experiences brought discouragement. I met several Quichua water technicians who had been trained by MAP. They were interested in doing health education in one community where they had helped install a gravity-fed water system. They had servants' hearts, and I was overjoyed to work with them. The last six months of my one-year grant was spent working primarily in that community.

An ad hoc committee was formed to improve the health and nutrition of the community, particularly for the children. To assess the community's nutritional status, the committee did a community survey of factors that affected food use. They took arm circumference measurements of all children under age five.

Most of my learning came through being with these people, listening to them talk about their lives, and asking questions. Eventually they began to ask questions about my life and my culture, which made me realize they were beginning to trust me. I began to see my role as a learner and an encourager, not as a teacher who was doing something for the community.

I laughed a lot with these new friends and enjoyed being with them. I learned to accept that I would never become one of them, that I would always be an outsider. In spite of our differences, we could laugh, cry, share life together, and learn from one another.

Embracing Change

As I worked through my discouragement, I had to learn how to feel my feelings, but with an openness to change and a teachable, listening spirit. My heart-searching reflection was often painful, particularly when it meant discovering things about myself that I preferred not to recognize. But after many months I saw growth coming from that reflection. Such reflection required an attitude of embracing change rather than fearing it, recognizing that God was working with me as a potter works with clay.

Sometimes we get set in our patterns of relating to God. When that relationship begins to grow and change, it can be difficult. When a potter wants to change something he or she has created, sometimes the potter lets the clay dry out, breaks the vessel into pieces, and grinds them into fine powder. The potter then adds water and gives life to the lifeless powder, making it into a workable mass of clay that can again be formed into a useful vessel.

I could identify with this process of drying out and being broken into pieces. It didn't make the process less painful, but it helped me understand what was happening to me. I began to hope again. I longed for the life-giving water to be added so that I could become a workable mass of clay, but I realized the Potter was in control of that. I had responsibilities in this process, but by refusing to make certain demands of myself, particularly in terms of my spirituality, I learned to be more open to change.

Finding Community

Another important part of my healing came through finding community among others who were struggling with similar issues. After my first year in Ecuador, I accepted a position with MAP in September 1986. It made a difference for me to work through the difficult issues of community development as a member of a team rather than on my own.

The richness of the team lies in its diversity. We represent various countries and cultures—Quichua Indians, *mestizos* from Ecuador and Colombia, and North Americans. We also represent many disciplines—agronomists, engineers, educators, nurses, nutritionists, physicians, and community development workers.

What draws this team together is a commitment to supporting the underprivileged of Ecuador in their efforts to lead healthier lives. This commitment has led to an involvement in water and sanitation projects, savings and loan cooperatives, family gardens, raising guinea pigs, nutrition and health education, and most recently, community-based primary health care.

The issues I face as an expatriate working in community health development have not gotten easier. But as part of a team I no longer feel alone in the struggle. I now work directly with four people—two Quichua women facilitators and two agronomists. We are supported by others at MAP who are trained in community health, nursing, medicine, and nonformal education. I depend on other members of the team for insight, opinions, and experiences related to our work together. I am learning how to receive criticism for my work and behavior without feeling destroyed.

Relationships Outside Work

In addition to finding community as part of a team, I found that forming several deep friendships with people outside my work life gave me a needed balance. It is impossible for me to compartmentalize my life into work life, social life, and spiritual life—since all are interrelated. However, when I noticed that almost all of my primary relationships were work-related, I saw that could easily prove to be unhealthy for me.

My Ecuadoran friends have taught me to *pasear* (to go out and be together—literally "to stroll"). This reduces my intensity. They also help keep my individualistic tendencies in check, as such qualities are not valued here as they are in the United States. I still remain a reflective person who needs time alone to "process" things, but I have come to appreciate groups for the support and healing they can provide. I have found that Ecuadorans have a lot to teach us *gringos* about what community is and how it can provide healing, peace, and joy in our lives.

I have also found writing letters to be a good way to express frustrations and hurts to those who can respond with insight, words of encouragement, or just expressions of concern.

Learning to Fly

As I look back on the past two-and-a-half years in Ecuador, I remember the pain, discouragement, and brokenness I experienced. Yet something has changed. When a friend asked me to sum up my last year, I told him that I had experienced the exhilaration of learning to fly—without taking aviation lessons!

I feel as if I have been set free from previous ideas, misconceptions, and hang-ups—all chains that kept me enslaved. I had been too serious, intense, and demanding of myself. Thanks to my Quichua friends, I am learning how to laugh. I have discovered a whole new world of potential and creativity.

Learning to fly involves taking risks, opening up, and letting go. Once you're in the air, it requires balance. I now have the freedom to feel all the feelings I have, freedom to embrace change rather than run from it, freedom in relationships. I now have a community with which I can laugh, dance, and experience all the richness of the world around me.

How do we deal with discouragement in cross-cultural service? Some leave in frustration. Others stick it out by sheer determination—but with a do-or-die mentality that may lead to denial of feelings or a resentment toward God and others.

There is a better way. Letting go of our perfectionist expectations of ourselves and affirming our own humanness, becoming a student of those we serve, embracing change, and entering into community both with co-workers and those outside the workplace— along this path lies healing. And wings.

Katie Pitkin is the coordinator of the Women-in-Development Program of MAP International in Ecuador, an integrated community development program aimed at improving the health of Quichua Indian families. She has lived in Ecuador for five and a half years.

17. One Master or Two: How Do We Measure Success?

by David Bosscher

> "I tell you the truth," Jesus replied, "no one who has left home or brothers or sisters or mother or father or children or fields for me and the gospel will fail to receive a hundred times as much in this present age . . . and in the age to come, eternal life." (Mark 10:29-30)

I NEVER THOUGHT much about success until a couple of years ago. I was working in a small town in the Mississippi Delta and really feeling down. It was so bad I couldn't even begin to count all the reasons I was dissatisfied with life.

But I knew one reason. Although my medical practice was serving the needs of poor people in that community and had been for five years, I was not enjoying the rewards of my hard work. My income was lower than during my residency. Ten years out of medical school, far from being financially set, I was discovering new financial worries. Our church seemed stuck. Our fellowship with a few of the folks was good, but almost nonexistent with the rest. People were avoiding my practice because they didn't want to rub shoulders with the poor. Overall, my life appeared a failure.

In contrast, other doctors in town whose "service to the poor" never seemed to go beyond writing off uncollectible debts were enjoying all the trappings of success. Respected, viewed as "the best doctors," financially secure, kids in good colleges—no one doubted they had everything going for them.

I asked myself if my work was worth it. I knew Christ had promised manifold rewards in this life, plus eternal life. I knew grubbing after money was not the way to happiness and that the rewards my fellow doctors were earning were treasures on earth that moths and rust could corrupt. I knew obedience to Christ was the standard by which Christians were to measure success or failure. I knew all that. Still I hurt. Either I was doing something wrong or I was not spiritual enough or committed enough.

Defining Success

My hurt got me thinking about success. Most North Americans define success in terms of tangible results. If someone asks us what we are doing, we share our latest degree or honor, the growth of our practice, our latest promotion, or the options on our newest car.

Even those of us who consciously reject that standard often unconsciously accept parts of it. I knew that the success of my fellow doctors in town was fleeting at best, yet I felt second-rate compared to them. I felt bad when patients with whom I had established good rapport during my on-call duty at the local hospital would not consider me for their physician because I was "the poor people's doctor."

I felt worried and angry when my practice struggled financially because it was committed to the poor and did not receive the usual guaranteed income from the hospital in town. At such times I found it difficult to hold onto the biblical definition of success.

When we don't conform to society's standard, we often feel like failures, although we know Christ measures success differently. If we work among the poor, this sense of failure may mean our service never goes beyond a clerkship, a rotation, or perhaps a few years of service. It was a rare week in which I did not consider moving on to something less draining.

The Pursuit of Success

The pursuit of success begins at the knees of our parents. Even in most Christian homes, there is little questioning of the American formula for success. Formal schooling rarely provides either teaching or role models to contradict the notion that successful people are those with the most visible achievements.

We often convince ourselves that we can at least appear successful in the world's eyes without compromising our Christian faith. We abandon neither our faith *nor* worldly success. We buy into them as separate packages and pursue them as parallel goals.

During medical training, for example, while we might not regularly play up to important faculty members, we still want to appear to be promising, young health professionals. We dress the part, we study to prove ourselves worthy of the part, and most of the time we go out of our way to act the part. Many of our

Christian role models and peers do the same. We do some things to pursue our Christian calling and others for the sake of worldly success.

At first neither road is particularly rocky. Because of our status as respected health care practitioners, we are considered "serious" Christians and frequently assume leadership roles in our churches. We take this as evidence that we are spiritually successful.

At the same time, we are maturing as professionals in a secular world. As we become more comfortable with our credentials as health care professionals, we might even share Christ with our patients or clients, but we avoid being blatant about it.

At times we are forced to make uncomfortable compromises—but not often enough to cause real disquiet. For many, one such compromise is the repayment of school loans. The popular wisdom is that our large debts force us to work in jobs where we can make real money until we make a dent in those loans. Then we can begin our service to the Lord. The calling to serve the Lord and our calling to serve our professional needs can easily be seen as separate.

J. I. Packer, in a *Christianity Today* editorial, says,

> Though we negate secular humanist doctrine, we live by its value system and suffer its symptoms: Man-centeredness as a way of life, with God there to care for me; preoccupation with wealth, luxury, success, and lots of happy sex as a means to my fulfillment; unconcern about self-denial, self-control, truthfulness, and modesty; high tolerance of moral lapses, with readiness to make excuses for ourselves and others in the name of charity. . . . Is any of that Christian? ("From the Senior Editor: Decadence à la Mode," October 2, 1987, p. 13)

Preparation for Service

John Perkins, founder of Voice of Calvary Ministries in Jackson, Mississippi, has said that ministries to the poor are best served by believers who commit themselves to single-minded, long-term service in a community of need. Short-term service can be helpful in some settings. But those health professionals whose shoes are nailed to the floor in poor communities will be able to best impact those communities. (See John Perkins, *Let Justice Roll Down*, Regal Books, 1976 and *With Justice for All*, Regal Books, 1982.)

Relating to poor people as brothers and sisters in Christ, understanding poverty and its impact on people, and exploring long-term solutions to the problems of poor communities take a long time.

How does our professional education prepare us for service to the poor? If it prepares us at all, it is likely to prepare us for short-term service. Anything more than that forces us to become too much of a fool for Christ. It might even cause others to view us as religious fanatics—an image incompatible with "success."

Nevertheless, some do commit to full-time, long-term service to the poor. They must constantly struggle with the tension between their callings and the shallow, largely secular definitions of success learned in school. My own struggle exemplifies this. Measured by that standard, serving the poor is probably the most unsuccessful pursuit I could have chosen.

Why do most people view service to the poor as a sign of failure? Part of the answer lies in the characteristics of many poor people who are without political influence, financially impoverished, and often members of minority groups. They are not the characters in most people's success stories.

Most North Americans suspect that if the poor

worked harder and quit having babies, they could pull themselves up by their own bootstraps. Their advice to me would be, "Use your training and experience among people who deserve it, who will appreciate what you have done for them, and who have the potential for some real change."

Living and working in an impoverished community is not easy for most of us. Expectations of rural bliss or urban diversity soon give way to harsh realities. For example, one reward I expected was appreciation from my patients. But few patients ever thanked me. In fact, the patients to whom I gave the most thanked me least. That bothered me, especially since I was not getting the financial rewards, the close fellowship, the stimulating cultural opportunities, or the honors.

Establishing a Faithful Path

We need to map out our road to success early, certainly no later than our professional training years. The longer we try to travel dual paths to success—one leading to secular goals and the other to spiritual goals —the more difficult it will be to embrace the unity Christ can bring to life.

Spiritual success is measured by the level of our obedience to the calling of Christ. "For whoever does the will of my Father in heaven is my brother and sister and mother" (Matt. 12:50). We must take the time to hear God. God can speak to us as we study the Word or hear it preached. Prayer enables us to know more fully the mind of Christ. And we need close fellowship with other believers who can help us connect God's Word with how we live. Unless we faithfully maintain these disciplines, our pursuit of godly success will meet with frustration and failure.

My wife and I recognized that we would eventually be tempted to ignore our desire to serve the poor. So we shared our vision to practice among underserved populations with anyone who would listen, even while we were in college and medical school. There would have been a lot of egg on our faces if we had reneged on our commitment! We particularly shared our vision with our families, both to gain their support and also to serve notice that we probably would not be setting up a practice down the street from them.

Our friends were primarily those who shared our vision. Often one of them would spend time in a ministry that served the poor, and we would benefit from their resulting insights. As we got to know each other better, we developed mutual accountability. That way, if one of us pursued goals inconsistent with our vision, our friends could confront us. We also sought out those who had served in nontraditional settings to learn about their struggles and joys in those settings.

I found it important to be part of a group consciously struggling with what it means to serve the poor and to sit at the feet of those who model service to the poor. Until I saw such ministry firsthand, I could not imagine how I could serve the poor with medical care and community development. After that experience, the challenges intimidated me, but I realized serving the poor through health care was a realistic goal.

Continuing to Challenge the World's Standard

The need to maintain spiritual disciplines is no less real for those who have completed their training. A common temptation at this stage is to give only a *portion* of our lives to the Lord's service, retaining the rest for pursuit of worldly success. If Christ's calling has taken us to communities of need, we may consider our service completed if we last a few years.

Even after living in a community of need for some years, however, there are struggles with success that I have not yet conquered. At the beginning, our practice income was so meager that I wondered what our family was going to live on. Though we never wanted for the necessities of life, it was difficult to trust God's providence for future needs, such as our daughters' college education. I often wished I had the easy financial success that attends most medical practices.

At other times I yearned for recognition. When I heard someone praising another physician in town, it hurt that they did not include me. In retrospect that seems petty, yet it goes back to how we perceive success. We want worldly *and* godly success, even though Christ says we cannot serve both God and mammon.

I finally came to the conclusion that no matter how well-prepared I was to serve the poor and how long I had lived in a poor community, I would always know times of discouragement and pain. This realization helped me seek assistance during those times and rest in the assurance that God would not place more on me than I could bear—or at least God would give me an out. I began to keep a journal that documented the low times and the ways God brought me out of my discouragement. Reviewing this journal helps me put things in perspective.

A physician who was setting up a clinic to serve the poor in Philadelphia once told me that ministry was impossible without high-quality fellowship and a strong support group. I disagreed with her at the time because in many communities such fellowship is simply unavailable. *Requiring* strong support and fellowship in the community of service limits the places Christians can serve.

Now, however, I am less certain of my position. Fellowship with other believers not only feeds our vision and holds us accountable; it also helps us through the discouraging times which distort our perception.

During the six years my family lived in Mississippi, God provided a succession of godly friends. One couple in particular provided a living example of what it meant to lay down their lives for Christ. Their encouragement strengthened and renewed us. My wife and I also discovered that our marriage and family life provided much of the perspective, creativity, and respite our work required. This allowed our relationship to grow along lines that would have been impossible without the struggles we experienced.

Although we could not always see this at the time, later we could look back and see God's care in our lives. We came to trust God more and to appreciate God's power more deeply. For example, when we were looking for a home, there were only one or two houses for sale. Just before we signed papers to rent a place that was reasonably priced but inadequate for our family, a house that exactly met our needs became available. This showed us that God cared about all our needs, not just the spiritual ones.

I can give personal testimony to the joy that comes from following Christ's calling, even when our life's goals seem folly to nonbelievers. It makes the happiness that depends on circumstances seem pale in comparison. And that, I think Jesus would say, is the fruit of true success.

David Bosscher, D.O., is teaching in a family practice residency at a community hospital in Midland, Michigan. Before that he was a family physician in the Mississippi Delta for six years.

18. Obedience and the Call to Serve the Poor

by David Caes

When they had finished eating, Jesus said to Simon Peter, "Simon son of John, do you truly love me more than these?"

"Yes, Lord," he said, "you know that I love you."

Jesus said, "Feed my lambs."

Again Jesus said, "Simon son of John, do you truly love me?"

He answered, "Yes, Lord, you know that I love you."

Jesus said, "Take care of my sheep."

The third time he said to him, "Simon son of John, do you love me?"

Peter was hurt because Jesus asked him the third time, "Do you love me?" He said, "Lord, you know all things: you know that I love you."

Jesus said, "Feed my sheep." (John 21:15-17)

ONE THEME that runs through the Gospels is obedience to God.

When the angel told Mary that she had been chosen

to bear the Christ-child, Mary responded, "I am the Lord's servant. . . . May it be to me as you have said" (Luke 1:38). Though she had just received news of something humanly impossible, she was willing to obey. Mary's simple faith took the angel at its word.

As twentieth-century Christians, we tend to regard the angel's announcement of the coming birth of Jesus as a quaint story, perhaps something we would teach in Sunday school. We gloss over the magnitude of this event. How would you respond if an unmarried woman came to your church or clinic and told such a story? I certainly would be skeptical! Yet the angel's announcement was no less amazing in that day than it would be in ours.

Complaining Obedience

Later we find Jesus preaching early one morning to a group of people in a town by the Lake of Gennesaret. While he was speaking, some fishermen came in with their boats and started cleaning their nets, probably listening to Jesus as they pulled away weeds and debris.

The crowd got so large that Jesus climbed into the prow of one of their fishing boats so everyone could see him. When he finished preaching, he told one fisherman, a man named Simon (Peter), to push the boat out into the water and throw out the nets.

Simon complained. He may have told Jesus how he had worked all night and was tired, how it was too late in the day to catch fish, how he had just finished cleaning his nets, and that he had just come in from fishing and hadn't had any luck.

But he had heard enough to know that Jesus spoke with authority. In fact, Simon called him, "Master." Reluctantly, he put the nets out—and was promptly overwhelmed by the catch. There were so many fish that the nets started to break and the boat almost capsized (Luke 5:1-5). Peter obeyed Jesus—but only after complaining about the inconvenience.

I wish I could say I have Mary's attitude, but I am more like Peter. I eventually obey Jesus. But not until I complain to God that it's a crazy idea, it won't work, I'm already overworked, and it's inconvenient.

I wonder if I have sometimes gotten so wrapped up in complaining that I have missed the blessing that comes in obeying God. If Simon Peter had kept complaining, Jesus probably would have shrugged his shoulders and walked away. It scares me to think of the times when I may have missed God's will completely because I was too busy complaining.

Our ultimate example of obedience is Jesus. The Gospels suggest that Jesus became increasingly aware that he was going to be killed rather than knowing it all along. He also seemed to know that his death would be excruciatingly painful, since he said, "But I have a baptism to undergo, and how distressed I am until it is completed!" (Luke 12:50).

On the Mount of Olives Jesus pleaded with God to "take this cup from me" (Luke 22:42), but when the time came, he submitted to God's will. Jesus struggled with his calling, but he obeyed.

Examples of Disobedience

Some people did not obey Jesus' calling. A rich ruler approached Jesus and asked how he could obtain eternal life. Jesus told him to "sell everything you have and give to the poor." It sounds like Jesus was inviting him to become one of the disciples, but the sticking point was that the rich man would not let go of his material possessions (Mark 10:17-23; Luke 18:18-25).

Jesus has a way of getting to the heart of the issue. He knew that the ruler was preoccupied with material wealth. Jesus knew that he would not give up his possessions in order to follow. This is an important story for us, since most Western Christians today encounter no greater stumbling block to obeying Christ than our desire to hold onto our material wealth.

One way we justify our wealth is by claiming to use it for the Lord's service. Some of us feel guilty about our lack of personal involvement. We try to soothe our consciences by throwing money at the ministry opportunities before us. While God does want our money, God is far more interested in our service. Gifts of money are no substitute for serving the Lord with our lives.

Some of us respond to the call to sell all by claiming we have a simpler lifestyle than those around us. But I know my simple lifestyle often becomes an end in itself rather than a means to serve God.

Despite our attempts to water down this saying of Jesus to sell all, it is something we must come to grips with. For those who call themselves disciples, the claims of God are nonnegotiable.

In Mark's account of this story, Peter adds, "We have left everything to follow you" (Mark 10:28). Evidently the disciples literally left everything behind—their homes, jobs, material possessions, even their families. When they joined the apostolic band, they may not have realized just how stringent the terms of entry into the kingdom were. Tradition says that all the disciples except John died of unnatural causes. Obedience to God costs our lives.

Luke also records the calling of several other people to be disciples. One man said he had to go back to bury his father. Another had to say good-bye to his family. Jesus' response was unyielding. "No one who puts his [or her] hand to the plow and looks back is fit for service in the kingdom of God" (Luke 9:62).

Jesus' audience would have understood this analogy immediately. You can't plow a straight furrow if you are always looking back; you have to watch where you are going. To follow Jesus, we must leave some things behind. A disciple who is always looking back to the life left behind is unfit for the kingdom. The work of the kingdom requires singleness of purpose.

Taking Up the Cross

Earlier in the same chapter Jesus says:

> If anyone would come after me, he must deny himself and take up his cross daily and follow me. For whoever wants to save his life will lose it, but whoever loses his life for me will save it. What good is it for [someone] to gain the whole world, and yet lose or forfeit his very self [soul]? If anyone is ashamed of me and my words, the Son of Man will be ashamed of him when he comes in his glory and in the glory of the Father and of the holy angels. (Luke 9:23-26, NRSV)

The imagery Jesus uses here is that of a public execution, a common occurrence in that time. The most common method of execution was crucifixion. The condemned person was forced to carry the crossbeam of the cross through the city streets on the way to the place of execution.

Jesus was clear about the costs of discipleship. He told his followers, "If you follow me, you could be killed." But he also told them that if they were ashamed of Jesus before others, then Jesus would be ashamed of them at his second coming.

These words of Jesus bear little resemblance to

much of the theology we hear today. Popular theology seems most concerned with making the hearer feel good. It talks about bringing Jesus into our lives, rather than bringing us into Jesus' life. It tells how Jesus can fulfill our lives, not how we can serve his kingdom. It ignores the cross and makes the gospel palatable.

We confidently assume that we know what is best for us and what we need to grow in faith. In practice that means we never do anything too uncomfortable, too risky, or too inconvenient. We have great plans for our own security and happiness. As long as we can, we try to control our lives. It is only when the situation gets desperate that we finally call on God. Only when everything else fails do we "let go and let God."

That was not Jesus' message. It was the devil who told Eve, and who whispers in our ear, "You will not . . . die" (Gen. 3:4). But Jesus tells us that to grow in faith is to embrace death—our own death.

Faith and Social Justice

When we speak of faith, most of us immediately think of a personal faith. But the Scriptures teach that a personal faith divorced from a commitment to social justice is a mockery.

The Mosaic Law contains special provisions for providing for the poor. It ensures that the poor always have access to the means of production. Isaiah, Amos, and Jeremiah rebuked oppressive affluence. David spoke of God vindicating the cause of the poor. The promise of the gospel announced by Mary speaks of a new order in human affairs (Luke 1:46-55).

Jesus said that his ministry was "to preach good news to the poor . . . to proclaim release to the captives and recovering of sight to the blind, to set at liberty those who are oppressed" (Isa. 61:1-2; Luke 4:18-19, RSV).

Jesus also says that our profession of love for God will be tested by our actions in feeding the hungry, clothing the naked, caring for the homeless, and ministering to the practical needs of the afflicted (Matt. 25:31-46). James warns that faith without works is dead (James 1:14-27).

"Woe to you Pharisees," Jesus warned, "because you give God a tenth of your mint, rue, and all other kinds of garden herbs, but you neglect justice and the love of God. You should have practiced the latter without leaving the former undone" (Luke 11:42). In the same breath Jesus condemned them for neglecting both justice and the love of God. You can't practice one without the other.

Numerous Scriptures refer to the oppressed, the alien, the orphan, and the widow—those at the bottom of the social structure. When the Son of God arrived on the scene, he went out to lunch with the rich every now and then, but he spent most of his time with the poor—those at the bottom. By his relationship to them, Jesus demonstrated their value in God's eyes. If Jesus identified with the poor, what does that mean for us?

Personal Relationships with the Poor

Most of us do not have relationships with the poor because we are far from them. Our society encourages us to isolate ourselves. Our suburbs do not just offer comfortable homes with green lawns and good schools nearby; they also insulate us from the poor.

Our highways let us travel through poverty-stricken neighborhoods without seeing the sights, hearing the sounds, and smelling the smells of poverty. Even many of us who live near poor people have nothing more than a superficial relationship with them.

Newspaper articles and television documentaries inform us and may shock us. They may even make us feel a little guilty for being relatively affluent. But they don't change our hearts.

The response that has been most popular with the political left has been to throw money at the poor. We have seen the rise of all kinds of social programs, which the political right has used for target practice. While some social programs have been helpful, they have not dealt with the root causes. One reason for this is that they tend to throw money at problems rather than promote personal involvement.

Apart from personal involvement with the poor, identification with the poor is impossible. And when affluent folks make friends among the poor, powerful changes can take place. Proximity to poor people is critical to our capacity for compassion.

The answer isn't for everyone to move into the inner city. The poor couldn't handle the inundation! However, unless we have relationships with poor people, we cannot listen to, learn from, or understand them.

Such relationships can be embarrassing to us professionals. After all, for years we have been cultivating this image of sophistication. What will our colleagues say, we fearfully wonder, if they hear we are spending time in a poor community? But is what others think really important in light of eternal values?

The Cost of Obedience

Occasionally I hear believers speak of the costs of serving God in the city. They fear for their personal safety, they can't find adequate housing, or they're worried about their children's schooling. I confess that it does get lonely serving God in the city. I hear my brothers and sisters serving in rural areas complain of feeling lonely, too.

I have come to believe that for every imprisoned person, drug-pusher, and unwed mother, there is someone called by God to proclaim God's love to that person and situation. If that is true, then why are our cities such a disaster? Why is crime so rampant? Why are so many people abusing themselves and others?

We can point to greed and racism, and those are part of the answer. But I suspect there is a deeper, more universal reason: most whom God has called are not obeying. God has called people with unique gifts to deal with those problems and proclaim the love of God in a fallen world—but they have turned a deaf ear.

Such disobedience is easy to understand. I can tell you this from personal experience. When you are all alone on your block and your house gets broken into for the third time, your car gets vandalized, some of your friends refuse to come visit because they fear for their personal (or their car's!) safety—then it's easy to understand why many disobey God's call.

Seeking the Heart of God

Many of us are middle-class; the majority of us are white. Most of us have not experienced the structural and personal oppression the poor live with day in and day out. But we have no cause to feel guilty about that. That is the way God brought us into the world. Barbara Williams-Skinner points out,

> Of all the revolutionary changes that have taken place in the world over time, there has never been a move-

ment that middle-class people have not headed, whether it is the civil rights movement, the peace movement, or movements for freedom in other countries. It takes people who eat three meals a day to worry about change. People who are worried about day-to-day survival and getting their next meal generally don't spend time dealing with the long-range changes in the social, political, and economic order, although they are oppressed by the existing order. ("Self-Care and Empowerment," *Health & Development*, Spring 1986, p. 6)

Our response must begin on our knees before God. Prayer humbles us. Through prayer the truth is revealed about ourselves and the choices we have made. As we confess and repent, we recall our identity as God's children. Our frame of reference is changed. Prayer gives us security in God to resist the false securities that lead us away from the path God calls us to.

To seek the heart of God, we must search Scripture. What does the Bible say about our relationships to the poor? How are we to treat the hungry or homeless? How did the Son of God spend his life on earth?

We must also seek out other Christians who desire to serve the poor. This provides not only a source of fellowship and support but also of accountability. If we are to be honest with ourselves and with God, we need other Christians to support us.

Then we must look for ways to develop relationships with the poor. We can volunteer our services at a social service ministry, even if we are only a student. We can talk to pastors of churches in poor communities and ask for suggestions. Many organizations that serve the poor need volunteers to work in housing programs, literacy tutoring programs, chaplaincy programs in local jails and prisons.

We must evaluate our career plans. Have our

choices excluded the poor? In our pursuit of security and happiness, have we neglected God's concern for the poor?

"Do You Love Me?"

After Jesus' second resurrection appearance to the disciples, seven of the disciples were out in a boat fishing all night, but they didn't catch a thing. They were almost back to the shore when a man on shore told them to throw their nets on the right side of the boat. They did—and caught 153 fish.

One of the other disciples yelled at Simon Peter, "It is the Lord." Simon Peter grabbed his coat, jumped into the water, and swam to shore (John 21:1-7).

Simon Peter had unfinished business with Jesus. After all, he had denied Christ three times. After Jesus served them breakfast, it sounds like Peter slipped away from the group. He loved Jesus, but it was painful to be around him after his denial. Jesus also slipped away and found Peter cleaning nets by the shore.

What followed must have been gut-wrenching for Simon Peter. It probably wasn't easy for Jesus either. Here was the man who had said he would go to prison or even die for Jesus. Yet when the chips were down, Peter denied even knowing Jesus. This was the first time Jesus and Peter had been alone together since the denial. It was the first opportunity for reconciliation.

Jesus asked, "Simon, do you love me more than these?" Exactly what Jesus meant by the question is unclear. But he may have been asking if Peter loved Jesus more than his fishing nets and all they represented. Peter responded, "You know that I love you."

There are two different Greek words translated "love" in this passage. The first is *agapao*, from the word *agape*. This means "sacrificial love." It is the love God showed in sacrificing his Son for us. Jesus used this word when asking Simon Peter if he loved him.

The second Greek word is *phileo*, meaning "to love as a friend." Simon Peter used the word *phileo* to respond to Jesus. Jesus asked if Simon Peter loved him with God's sacrificial love. Peter responded by saying, "Yes, I am your friend." Jesus must have been hurt by this, but he told Simon Peter, "Feed my lambs."

I imagine that Peter couldn't even look Jesus in the eye. He was looking at the ground, pretending to be preoccupied with his nets. Jesus asked Peter a second time, "Simon son of John, do you love me?" Peter responded, "Yes, Lord, you know that I am your friend." Jesus told Simon Peter again, "Take care of my sheep."

The third time Jesus asked, "Simon . . . do you love me?" he switched to the word for "friend" that Simon Peter had been using. The Scriptures tell us that Peter was hurt because Jesus asked him the third time. Perhaps he was reminded of his three denials.

At that point he probably put down what he was doing and looked Jesus in the eye for the first time. "Lord, you know everything there is to know about me," he said. "You know that I am your friend."

Although Simon Peter had used the word "friend" throughout, perhaps because he felt ashamed and unworthy, Jesus was satisfied with his confession. "Feed my sheep," Jesus responded, and at that moment, Simon Peter was reconciled to Jesus (John 21:15-17).

Will You Serve Me?

Jesus' question to Peter is the same question Jesus asks each of us. He is looking us in the eye and asking, "Do you love me more than these? Do you love me more than your profession, salary, stature in the community? Will you serve me through serving 'the least of these brothers and sisters of mine,' even if it is embarrassing and inconvenient? Even if your colleagues scorn you because you serve God among the poor? Will you serve me—no matter what the cost?"

David Caes is the executive director of the Christian Community Health Fellowship.

Christian Community Health Fellowship

THE CHAPTERS of this book were written by members of the Christian Community Health Fellowship (CCHF). CCHF was formed to encourage Christian health professionals and others to develop effective approaches to meeting the health care needs of underserved areas in the United States. Central to our work is the call to live out the Gospel of Jesus Christ through health care among the poor.

CCHF publishes a quarterly, *Health and Development*, in addition to sponsoring several workshops each year. CCHF also sponsors and publishes a directory of sites where health care students can do a rotation with a Christian health professional who is working among the poor.

The founders of CCHF were very intentional when they chose the name

> **Christian.** We are believers in Jesus Christ. While the members of CCHF come from many different faith

traditions, it is because of Christ that we serve among the poor.

Community. If we are going to be effective in addressing the needs of the poor, we have to go to the communities where they are and address their felt needs.

Health. We seek to address the person as a whole person including their spiritual needs and not simply address the medical portion of a person's life.

Fellowship. Without the fellowship of one another, we would not be able to continue with our work.

If you would like additional information about CCHF, contact:

Christian Community Health Fellowship
803 N. 64th Street
P.O. Box 12548
Philadelphia, PA 19151-0548
215 877-1200

The Editor

DAVID CAES is executive director of the Christian Community Health Fellowship and has worked with CCHF since 1985.

He previously worked as an editor developing literary materials for Contemporary books, helped inmates at Cook County Jail in Chicago prepare for the high school equivalency test, and taught elementary school for five years.

David received a B.A. in education from Wheaton College (Ill.) in 1976; an M.Ed. from National College of Education (Evanston, Ill.) in 1980, and an M.B.A. from Eastern College (St. Davids, Pa.) in 1988.

He lives in Philadelphia, Pennsylvania, with his wife, Libby (Werenfels), and their daughter Amy (1985). They are members of West Philadelphia Mennonite Fellowship.